Ian McKellen: Extraordinary Life and Career

The official tribute to the world's theatre and film icon

Henry Lyle Donovan

Introduction

Ian McKellen is a legendary figure in show business, with a career that spans more than six decades and has left an indelible mark on theatre and film. Loved and respected by both his colleagues and audiences, McKellen has become synonymous with artistic excellence, versatility and social commitment. From his childhood in Burnley, scarred by the Second World War, to his triumphant performances on stage and screen, McKellen has turned every role into an opportunity to explore the complexity of the human condition. He is an actor capable of embodying both the tragic depth of Shakespearean characters and the epic power of modern cinema's heroes and antagonists, making each of his performances unique and unforgettable. This book pays tribute to Ian McKellen not only as an actor, but as a man of culture and activist. His life has been a constant search for truth and authenticity, both on and off stage. His work with Shakespeare has made him one of the greatest contemporary interpreters of the classics, but it was his ability to bring this same intensity to highly successful films, such as 'Lord of the Rings' and 'X-Men', that made him a global icon. In addition to his extraordinary artistic career, McKellen has distinguished himself for his commitment to civil rights battles, becoming one of the most influential voices in the LGBTQ+ community and using his fame to promote a more just and inclusive society. Through the pages of this tribute, we will explore McKellen's career in all its facets: from humble beginnings to major international successes, from memorable collaborations with world-renowned directors and actors to the personal challenges that have transformed him into an inspirational figure for millions. We will discover how his talent, determination and passion for art helped revolutionise the world of theatre and cinema, and how his commitment to social justice left an indelible mark on the hearts of those who followed him. This is a journey through the life and career of a man who knew how to combine art and activism, without ever losing his humility and his love for what he does.

-Arguments-

Chapter 1. The origins of Ian McKellen

Ian McKellen was born on 25 May 1939 in Burnley, a town in Lancashire, England, at a time in history deeply marked by the events of the Second World War. The war was a constant backdrop in his childhood, influencing his way of perceiving the world and partly shaping the thoughtful and profound character that would later characterise his artistic personality. During his growing years, the presence of war and its consequences were always vivid in his memory, not only because of the atmosphere of uncertainty and fear that pervaded everyday life, but also because of the awareness that the previous generation had experienced dramatic and complex events. Ian's family, although from a modest background, always valued education and culture, instilling in him a great love of literature and theatre from a young age. His father, Denis Murray McKellen, a civil engineer, and his mother, Margery Lois Sutcliffe, a housewife, were key figures in young Ian's education. His mother, in particular, shared with her son a passion for reading and the arts, and it is likely that she was the first to recognise her son's talent and artistic inclination.

Theatre entered Ian McKellen's life during his school years. Even as a child, McKellen showed a keen imagination and a natural inclination for acting. His discovery of his love for the theatre came about thanks to a key event: his parents' gift of a toy theatre, with which young Ian began staging his first home performances. This toy theatre became his creative refuge, a space where he could freely express his imagination and begin to experience the deeper meaning of storytelling. The spark of his passion for acting was ignited by seeing a play in Manchester when McKellen was still a boy. That moment, watching the actors on stage, was revelatory for him: he realised that this was the path he wanted to take. Theatre soon became for Ian not only a passion, but a way of interpreting the world and confronting the big questions of human existence, an interest that would accompany him throughout his life.

During his teenage years, McKellen attended Bolton School, a prestigious school where he found teachers who encouraged him to develop his talent for acting. The school environment was conducive to artistic exploration, and it was here that McKellen began participating in his first plays. Every school play, every scene he performed, confirmed in him his love of theatre. Those years were also marked by a deep intellectual curiosity, with McKellen immersing himself in the study of literary classics, particularly the works of Shakespeare. The English playwright exerted a special fascination on him, not only for the complexity of his characters, but for the depth of the moral and human issues addressed in his texts. His encounter with Shakespeare marked a crucial turning point in Ian's life, as he began to see theatre not only as a means of artistic expression, but as a tool for exploring the human condition. The influence of McKellen's family was instrumental not only in sustaining his artistic inclination, but also in creating an environment of great open-mindedness and moral support. The tragic death of his mother when Ian was just 12 years old left a huge void in his life, but at the same time strengthened his bond with his father and sister Jean. Denis McKellen, although a practical and rational man, never hesitated to support his son in his desire to become an actor. This trust and encouragement were essential for the young McKellen, who began to see theatre not only as a creative refuge, but also as a way to confront and overcome personal traumas and life's difficulties.

The love of theatre and family influence combined to forge in McKellen an extraordinary determination. After high school, he decided to pursue his academic and theatrical studies in Cambridge, at St. Catharine's College, an institution that has trained some of the most brilliant minds in British theatre. At Cambridge, McKellen became fully immersed in academia and theatre, participating in numerous university productions that brought him into contact with future greats of British theatre. It was during this period that McKellen consolidated his idea of becoming a professional actor, finding in his fellow students and teachers the first mentors and colleagues with whom he could share his passion. The Cambridge years were not only a time of artistic growth, but also of personal discovery. Here, McKellen found the intellectually stimulating environment he was seeking, and was able to explore in depth the meaning of acting and the actor's moral responsibility in bringing great human truths to the stage.

During his university years, Ian McKellen realised that his destiny was inextricably linked to the theatre. His first experiences on stage were greeted with enthusiasm and, after graduation, there was no doubt that acting would be his path. He immediately started working with some of the most important British theatre companies, working his way up through the ranks and gaining experience. His dedication and talent did not go unnoticed, and soon McKellen began to make a name for himself in the British theatre scene. What began as a youthful love for the theatre had turned into a full-fledged vocation, sustained by his innate talent and the unwavering support of his family, who, despite the difficulties, had always believed in him.

Ian McKellen's origins are thus intertwined with the story of his love for theatre, a love that accompanied him from an early age and that defined his entire existence. The support of his family, his formative experiences at school, and his immersion in the academic world of Cambridge have helped shape the character and career of one of the most loved and respected actors of our time. McKellen was able to turn his passion into a brilliant career, always keeping firmly rooted in the love of theatre that he discovered at a young age and that would guide him throughout his life.

Chapter 2. The discovery of theatre

The discovery of theatre for Ian McKellen was an experience that profoundly marked his life and laid the foundations for a career destined to become legendary. From a young age, McKellen found himself immersed in a world of stories and imagination, fascinated by the infinite possibilities of expression offered by the stage. His first school plays represented for him a window into a universe in which he could explore new roles, emotions and realities. During his elementary and middle school years, he enthusiastically participated in school productions, discovering that acting allowed him to bring to life characters that he had only imagined until then. In those early years, every performance was a discovery for him, a new opportunity to experience the transformative power of theatre. Acting made him feel alive, connected to a larger dimension, where he could put his whole self into play, both physically and emotionally. And while other kids were dabbling in sports or recreational activities, McKellen found solace in taking refuge in the folds of ancient and universal stories, glimpsing a future that bound him inextricably to the theatre.

McKellen's bond with theatre was strengthened during his teenage years, when he had his first encounter with William Shakespeare. It was the Bard's work that completely captured his imagination, opening up new horizons for young

Ian, who immediately felt drawn to the depth of the characters and complexity of the themes dealt with in Shakespeare's plays. The Shakespearean language, with its rhythm and musicality, became a kind of second language for McKellen, a vehicle through which he could express his deepest emotions. Despite his young age, he was able to grasp the power and beauty of Shakespeare's writing, and it was through his plays that McKellen began to develop a deeper understanding of theatre as a means to explore the human condition. The tragic nature of Hamlet, the majesty of Macbeth, the madness of King Lear: each of Shakespeare's characters represented a world for McKellen to explore, an opportunity to challenge himself and grow as an actor and as a person. His love for Shakespeare was not just a momentary infatuation, but a bond that would accompany him throughout his life and profoundly influence his artistic journey. At school, McKellen was immediately noticed for his natural talent. Every performance, even in the most modest school plays, saw him excel over his peers, with a natural ability to interpret roles and capture the audience's attention. Despite the shyness that characterised his personality offstage, once on stage McKellen was transformed, bringing out a magnetic presence and emotional intensity that surprised teachers and classmates alike. His first school performances, albeit amateurish, were the perfect testing ground to develop his interpretative skills, refine his sense of rhythm and dialogue, and experiment with his body and voice, elements that would become fundamental tools of his art. His teachers soon recognised an uncommon talent in him, and it was thanks to their encouragement that McKellen began to see acting not just as a pastime, but as a true vocation. He attended every play with such commitment and dedication that it was clear that this boy had a bright future ahead of him.

Parallel to his discovery of school theatre, McKellen began to nourish himself with artistic influences that gave him further inspiration to develop his acting style. He grew to admire legendary actors of the British theatre, such as Laurence Olivier and John Gielgud, who represented true models of theatrical virtue for him. Olivier, with his ability to completely transform himself for each role, and Gielgud, a master of language and speech, became examples for McKellen to follow. Careful observation of their performances taught him the importance of preparation, discipline and the constant search for truth in the characters. McKellen soon realised that acting was not just a technical skill, but an act of deep empathy for the character, a spiritual connection that required dedication and honesty. These actors represented the benchmark for what McKellen hoped to one day become: a performer capable of touching the audience's deepest emotional chords and leaving an indelible mark through his performances.

As his exposure to theatre increased, McKellen began to outline what would be his future path. Every school performance, every retelling of Shakespeare's plays, only strengthened in him the conviction that theatre would be his destiny. It was during this period that McKellen began to dream big, imagining himself one day on prestigious stages, playing the great roles of the classical repertoire. The beginning of his dream of becoming a professional actor took shape slowly but surely, as young Ian deepened his knowledge of theatre and developed a mastery of acting techniques that set him apart from his peers. The enthusiasm he felt for acting became his driving force, pushing him to continually seek new opportunities to improve and challenge himself.

His love for Shakespeare and classical theatre did not, however, distract him from his curiosity about more modern forms of drama. Thus, in addition to the Shakespearean repertoire, McKellen also began to explore contemporary theatre, discovering authors such as Samuel Beckett and Harold Pinter, who offered new approaches to storytelling and interpretation. His eagerness to experiment and explore every aspect of acting demonstrated a deep thirst for knowledge and a tireless passion for the dramatic art at an early age. Each new text, each new performance, was for McKellen an opportunity to broaden his cultural and artistic background, preparing him for a career that would embrace both classical theatre and the new frontiers of drama.

The discovery of theatre represented for Ian McKellen not only the beginning of a brilliant career, but also a personal fulfilment, a way to fully express his own identity and worldview. Every step he took on stage brought him closer to his dream of becoming one of the most loved and respected performers in British theatre. And as the years passed and McKellen honed his talent, theatre was transformed from a simple passion into a true mission, beginning a journey that would lead him to become one of the greatest actors of his time.

Chapter 3. The formative years at Cambridge

Ian McKellen's formative years at Cambridge marked a crucial phase in his artistic evolution, a period in which the actor honed his talent and began to outline the extraordinary career that would make him one of the greatest theatre and film performers of his time. McKellen arrived at St. Catharine's College, Cambridge, with great enthusiasm and a strong desire to fully explore the academic and theatrical world. It was in this context that he encountered an intellectual and artistic community that stimulated him and brought him into contact with young actors and directors destined to profoundly influence British theatre. At Cambridge, McKellen found a lively and dynamic environment where theatre was not just a form of entertainment, but a way of life, a platform for exploring complex ideas, challenging conventions and expressing individuality. In those years, the university was a hotbed of emerging talent, and McKellen immersed himself completely in this environment, absorbing every experience and using every opportunity to improve his acting skills. McKellen's academic journey at Cambridge was not an easy one. The rigorous nature of university studies required iron discipline, and McKellen had to balance academic demands with his growing passion for theatre. Nevertheless, he managed to excel in both spheres, demonstrating uncommon determination and commitment. St. Catharine's College became the place where McKellen could deepen not only his literary and historical knowledge, but also the theatrical techniques and theories that would form the basis of his career. The courses he took, which focused on Shakespeare, the Greek classics and modern literature, helped to refine his understanding of the narrative structures and emotional dynamics that animate great dramatic works. This academic background proved fundamental to his growth as an actor, as McKellen did not want to limit himself to being a performer: he aspired to fully understand the texts he brought to the stage in order to deliver more authentic and insightful performances.

One of the most significant moments of his time at Cambridge was his encounter with the university theatre scene, a microcosm of creativity and innovation that allowed young actors to experiment without the restrictions of professional theatre. Here, McKellen found himself immersed in a community of passionate artists with whom he shared a love of acting and a desire to experiment with new approaches to drama. The university productions in which he participated during these years allowed him to test himself in a variety of roles, honing his technical skills and his ability to handle complex characters. McKellen quickly distinguished himself for his versatility, interpretative intelligence and extraordinary stage presence. It was evident that, even in an environment rich in talent, McKellen possessed something unique: a keen sensitivity and emotional depth that made him capable of bringing characters of great complexity to life with a naturalness that impressed colleagues and audiences alike.

During his years at Cambridge, McKellen also had the opportunity to engage with Shakespeare's repertoire in an extremely stimulating academic and artistic context. He participated in numerous university productions of Shakespeare, honing his interpretative style and gaining a deeper and deeper understanding of the Bard's works. Shakespeare, who had fascinated him from an early age, became a constant source of inspiration for McKellen. Every time he tackled one of his texts, he felt closer to the true essence of theatre, that ability to explore human emotions and experiences in all their complexity. The Shakespearean roles he played at Cambridge - including Hamlet, Macbeth and Richard III - were valuable opportunities to develop his approach to the great tragic characters, which required an enormous command of language and intense psychological understanding.

It was in this environment of experimentation and collaboration that McKellen formally debuted in the theatre, marking his first contact with professionalism. Although university productions did not have the same scope as professional theatre, they were an important training ground for honing skills in acting, directing and set design. McKellen realised that theatre was more than just an artistic expression: it was a discipline that required dedication, commitment and a constant search for emotional truth. His early theatre experiences at Cambridge prepared him for his later entry into the world of professional theatre, where he would continue to grow as an artist and explore new interpretative horizons.

Another key aspect of the Cambridge years was meeting future greats of British theatre and film. McKellen formed friendships and collaborations with other students who, like him, shared a passion for theatre and would go on to equally brilliant careers. This exchange of ideas and influences contributed to a climate of continuous artistic and intellectual growth. McKellen learned early on that theatre is a team effort, requiring perfect harmony between actors, directors, set designers and technicians. These human and professional relationships built during his university years represented an invaluable resource for his career, and many of those friendships continued over time, nurturing future collaborations in theatre and film.

The university experience, with its academic and artistic challenges, consolidated in McKellen the conviction that acting was his true vocation. The theatre productions in which he participated, the contact with classical texts, the intellectual discussions with colleagues and professors: all helped to forge the artist he was becoming. It was during this period that McKellen became more aware of the power of theatre as a medium to tell stories and explore universal themes, a lesson he would carry with him throughout his career. At Cambridge, the actor began to develop the discipline and dedication that would characterise his approach to his work for the rest of his life. His official theatrical debut during these years was only the first step in a long career that would lead him to worldwide acclaim.

Ian McKellen's first contact with professional theatre during his years at Cambridge was a moment of great significance. Although still a student, McKellen showed that he already possessed an uncommon artistic maturity, capable of tackling challenging roles with a depth and passion that impressed audiences and critics alike. This training period was crucial for his artistic growth, but also for the development of his self-confidence as an actor. Each performance, each scene he played in Cambridge, reinforced in him the conviction that theatre was the place where he could fully express his talent and his worldview. And so, with a wealth of educational experience and an ever-growing passion, Ian McKellen prepared himself for the world of professional theatre, ready to turn his youthful dreams into an extraordinary and unparalleled career.

Chapter 4. First theatrical successes

After completing his studies at Cambridge, Ian McKellen was now ready to enter the world of professional theatre. His academic training and university theatre experience had given him the confidence to take on new challenges, and the next step was joining a repertory company, an environment where young actors like himself could hone their acting skills. Repertory companies offered actors the chance to perform in a variety of roles, often with short intervals between productions, forcing them to move quickly from one character to another. This fast pace constituted an ideal school for McKellen, who learned to handle the complexity of the characters and to find new interpretative nuances in each role. His love of classical theatre, particularly Shakespeare, led him to immerse himself completely in the texts, exploring the language, emotions and psychology of the characters in depth. Working in a repertory company allowed him to build a solid technical foundation, challenging him with a variety of roles, from young tragic heroes to more mature and complex characters.

One of the first Shakespearean roles played by McKellen was that of Henry V, a character requiring great charisma and inner strength. His portrayal of the young English king immediately struck the critics with its intensity and his ability to convey both the heroism and vulnerability of the character. McKellen succeeded in bringing out the complexity of the sovereign, a man torn between duty and his own personal doubts, and his performance was appreciated for the maturity with which he tackled such a demanding role. This early success was a sign that McKellen was destined to become one of the most promising actors of his generation. His love for Shakespeare was not limited to the simple interpretation of the texts: McKellen saw in the Bard an inexhaustible source of human knowledge, an author capable of exploring the depths of the soul and offering his actors the opportunity to confront the most universal themes, such as love, power, revenge and redemption.

McKellen's talent for tragic roles was further consolidated with his portrayal of Richard III, one of the most complex and fascinating characters in Shakespeare's repertoire. Richard III is an ambiguous, manipulative and cruel character, but at the same time endowed with a dark charisma that captivates the audience. McKellen, with his extraordinary ability to enter the characters' psyche, gave life to an unforgettable Richard, a man dominated by ambition and the thirst for power, but at the same time aware of his own inevitable downfall. Critics were unanimous in recognising his ability to humanise such a complex and morally questionable character, and his performance became a benchmark for actors who would later tackle the role. McKellen had found fertile ground in Shakespeare to develop his talent, and it was through these early roles that he gained the attention of critics and audiences alike.

In addition to Shakespeare, McKellen tried his hand at other authors of classical theatre, expanding his repertoire and demonstrating his versatility as an actor. He participated in productions of Greek authors, such as Sophocles and Euripides, tackling roles that required a great ability to interpret pain, despair and tragedy. These characters, often marked by fate and unresolvable inner conflicts, allowed McKellen to explore new dimensions of acting, challenging himself with texts that required great emotional and physical control. His dedication and commitment to doing justice to each character did not go unnoticed, and before long McKellen established himself as one of the most interesting emerging actors in British theatre.

Critical recognition came quickly, thanks to his combination of natural talent, technical preparation and a deep respect for the theatrical text. Each of his performances was characterised by a maniacal attention to detail and a constant search for the emotional truth of the character. McKellen was never satisfied with a superficial or academic performance: his goal was always to go beyond the written text, to explore the characters' innermost motivations and to offer the audience a unique and personal vision of each role. This relentless pursuit of perfection soon made him a favourite of theatre directors, who saw in him a performer capable of tackling the most difficult challenges with great professionalism and passion.

McKellen's passion for classical theatre was evident in every role he played. For him, performing Shakespeare or the great Greek authors was not just a job, but a mission, an opportunity to confront the great questions of human existence and to share the cathartic experience of theatre with the audience. McKellen saw the stage as a sacred place, an environment where actors and spectators could connect on a deep level, through the sharing of emotions and universal stories. This conception of theatre as a noble and deeply human art guided his every performance, making him a performer capable of touching the most intimate chords of the human soul.

Another fundamental element of his early theatrical career was his ability to move with ease from tragic to comic roles, demonstrating an uncommon versatility. McKellen, in fact, did not limit himself to dramatic characters: with the same mastery he tackled light and brilliant roles, giving the audience moments of pure fun and lightness. This ability to move between different genres, without ever losing intensity or credibility, made him a complete and highly regarded actor throughout the British theatre scene. McKellen's early theatrical successes were thus the result of constant and passionate work, an unconditional love for theatre and a dedication that pushed him to continually improve.

McKellen's journey in repertory companies, enriched by his first Shakespearean roles and critical recognition, marked the beginning of a career destined to reach extraordinary heights. His passion for classical theatre, combined with his ability to play complex characters with depth and intensity, allowed him to build a solid and respected reputation. Each performance was an opportunity to explore new aspects of acting and to test his talent, and McKellen never failed to seize these opportunities with enthusiasm and humility. The early years of his acting career were, therefore, a period of exponential growth, during which McKellen laid the foundations to become the theatre and film icon we all know today.

Chapter 5. Consecration as a Shakespearean actor

Ian McKellen's consecration as a Shakespearean actor came when his name began to resonate strongly in British theatres, thanks to masterful interpretations of some of the most iconic roles in William Shakespeare's play. Two of the characters that were instrumental in defining him as one of Shakespeare's finest performers were Hamlet and Macbeth. These roles required not only a thorough knowledge of the texts, but also an extraordinary ability to immerse himself in the complex and often dark psychology of the characters. Hamlet, the tormented prince meditating on life and death, and Macbeth, the general consumed by ambition and guilt, represented immense challenges for any actor, but McKellen was able to tackle them with a depth and intensity that left a mark on audiences and critics alike. His interpretation of Hamlet was distinguished by the elegance and sensitivity with which he was able to make the Danish prince's existential musings tangible. McKellen did not just play the role: he embodied the character's emotional fragility, giving life to a Hamlet that oscillated between inner torment and cold rationality, offering the audience a version of the character that seemed more contemporary, while remaining faithful to the spirit of the original text.

Hamlet's performance not only confirmed McKellen as an exceptionally talented actor, but also earned him his first international critical accolades. Audiences were fascinated by his ability to make lines that had been recited hundreds of times by other actors before him seem new and fresh. He was able to infuse each monologue with a depth that made Hamlet himself seem to be in direct dialogue with the audience, rather than lost in thought. This intimacy with the text and mastery of the stage became McKellen's trademark. Critics acclaimed him for his ability to give the character a deeply human dimension, making Hamlet not only a young prince seeking revenge, but also a man reflecting on the meaning of life and the weight of fate. His interpretation was considered revolutionary for the way he managed to combine tradition with a more modern and universal sensibility, making the character accessible to a wider audience.

After the success of Hamlet, McKellen devoted himself to another of Shakespeare's great roles, playing Macbeth, one of the darkest and most fascinating characters in the theatre repertoire. Macbeth is a man devoured by ambition, whose thirst for power leads him into a spiral of violence and self-destruction. McKellen was able to capture the character's many layers of complexity with great effectiveness, conveying Macbeth's progressive moral and psychological disintegration as the story progresses. His performance was characterised by a rare emotional power and a physicality that made the character's inner conflict palpable. Macbeth's escalating madness, his descent into terror and despair, were rendered by McKellen with such intensity that the audience could not help but be fascinated and disturbed at the same time. The 'tomorrow and tomorrow and tomorrow' monologue, reflecting on the futility of existence, became one of the most memorable moments of his career, thanks to McKellen's ability to bring out not only the character's despair, but also his awareness of his own imminent end.

McKellen's connection with the Royal Shakespeare Company (RSC) was consolidated during this period, making him one of the most respected and sought-after actors in the British theatre scene. The RSC represented the temple of Shakespearean theatre, and performing in its prestigious theatres meant being part of the UK's theatrical elite. McKellen earned the respect of colleagues and directors alike through his professional seriousness and tireless pursuit of perfection. His dedication to his craft was evident in every performance, and his constant interaction with some of the greatest performers and directors of the time only fuelled his growth as an artist. Working with high-calibre directors, such as Peter Hall and Trevor Nunn, was fundamental to the development of his career, allowing him to explore new interpretative perspectives and experiment with different modes of expression. These directors recognised in McKellen a unique combination of talent, intelligence and passion, and chose him to play increasingly complex and challenging roles. International critics began to pay increasing attention to McKellen, recognising him as one of the most powerful voices in contemporary Shakespearean theatre. His roles in Hamlet and Macbeth were enthusiastically reviewed throughout Europe, and his reputation crossed British borders, making him a leading figure in world theatre. His ability to combine rigorous acting, grounded in years of study and practice, with a modern, accessible sensibility made him a beloved actor not only by educated, academic audiences, but also by new generations of spectators approaching theatre for the first time. McKellen was able to transform Shakespeare into something alive, relevant and vibrant, breaking down the barriers between classical theatre and contemporary sensibilities.

The consecration as a Shakespearean actor, however, was not an achievement for McKellen, but rather a starting point for an ever-evolving career. Despite his successes, he never stopped looking for new challenges and new modes of expression. His love for Shakespeare remained a constant throughout his career, but McKellen continued to explore other avenues as well, taking on different roles and constantly challenging himself. The depth of his interpretation of characters such as Hamlet and Macbeth was not only the result of years of study and practice, but also of an insatiable curiosity about the human soul, which McKellen was able to convey with a unique sincerity and vulnerability.

His work with the Royal Shakespeare Company made him one of the most respected actors in British theatre, and his performances of Shakespeare were considered among the most incisive and memorable of his generation. International critics acclaimed him as one of the Bard's great interpreters, capable of breathing new life into texts that, for many, represented the pinnacle of dramatic art. Thanks to roles such as Hamlet and Macbeth, McKellen became an indispensable figure of Shakespearean theatre, consecrated not only by public success, but also by critical acclaim and the respect of his colleagues.

Chapter 6. The transition to cinema

Ian McKellen's transition from theatre to film was a natural one, but not without its challenges. After establishing himself as one of the greatest theatrical actors of his time, mainly thanks to his Shakespearean interpretations, McKellen began to explore the possibilities offered by the big screen. His talent for acting had already been widely recognised on stage, but film represented a different terrain, with completely different dynamics, timing and approaches. Unlike theatre, where each performance is a unique and unrepeatable act, film requires technical precision, meticulous attention to detail, and the ability to adapt to repeated takes and precise directorial directives. McKellen realised early on that the transition from theatre to film would not be automatic: he would have to learn to modulate his performance, finding a balance between the theatrical energy and the delicacy required for the camera. Nevertheless, this challenge represented an extraordinary opportunity for McKellen to expand his repertoire and bring his acting style to a wider audience.

His early film experiences were characterised by small roles that, although they did not have the importance or visibility of his stage performances, allowed him to familiarise himself with the medium and develop a sense of comfort in front of the camera. One of his first significant roles was in 'A Touch of Love' (1969), where he starred alongside Sandy Dennis. Although the film did not make much of an impact on audiences, McKellen immediately demonstrated his ability to transport the depth and complexity of his theatrical characters into the cinematic context. Critics noted his talent, praising the naturalness with which he was able to move from the stage to the big screen, while maintaining his interpretative intensity. However, in spite of these early attempts, McKellen remained primarily bound to the theatre, where he felt he could best express his artistry.

The real turning point for McKellen's film career came with his performance in 'Richard III' (1995). The film, directed by Richard Loncraine, was a modern adaptation of Shakespeare's tragedy of the same name, set in a hypothetical 1930s England dominated by a fascist dictatorship. McKellen not only played the lead role, but also contributed to the script, adapting the Shakespearean text to make it more accessible and relevant to a contemporary audience. This version of 'Richard III' was an extraordinary success, both critically and with audiences, and marked McKellen's definitive establishment as a world-class film actor. His portrayal of Richard, the cruel and manipulative Duke of Gloucester who ascends the throne through a series of murders and betrayals, was acclaimed for its intensity and his ability to render the character simultaneously repulsive and fascinating. The film proved that McKellen was able to transpose his theatrical mastery into the cinematic context without losing the complexity and emotional power that had made him famous on stage. In 'Richard III', McKellen was able to take full advantage of the possibilities offered by the cinematic medium, using close-ups and direct glances at the camera to create an intimate and unsettling connection with the audience. His acting was less explosive than what he might have used on stage, but for this very reason it was even more effective: every gesture, every word, was charged with meaning, and the audience was captivated by his magnetic presence. His version of Richard III was not just a Shakespearean tyrant, but a universal symbol of corrupt power and unbridled ambition, echoed in the dictatorships and tyrannies of the 20th century. The success of 'Richard III' not only established McKellen as a leading film actor, but also made him known to an international audience that may not have had the opportunity to see him on stage. The film was screened at major film festivals around the world, garnering numerous awards and critical praise. Thanks to this performance, McKellen also obtained several nominations for the most prestigious awards, consolidating his status as a star not only in theatre, but also in film. However, despite his success, McKellen never gave up his passion for theatre: he continued to perform regularly on British stages and explore new roles, proving that film, although fascinating, would never completely supplant theatre in his life.

McKellen's transition from theatre to film represented a phase of great artistic growth for him. While cinema allowed him to reach a much wider audience, it also offered him new expressive possibilities that theatre, with its rigid rules and physical distance from the audience, could not give him. Cinema allowed him to explore the subtlety of gestures, the precision of facial expressions, and to fully exploit the power of images and editing to enrich his performances. However, the difference between the two worlds was obvious: whereas theatre requires a constant stage presence and the ability to capture the audience's attention for hours, cinema relies on fragments of scenes, shot at different times, which are then assembled to create the illusion of continuity. This change required McKellen to adapt his style, modulating his energy and learning to work with the camera differently than he had always done on stage.

Despite initial difficulties, McKellen managed to find his balance between these two worlds, bringing to film the same intensity and emotional depth that characterised his stage performances. His ability to switch between mediums with ease made him one of the most versatile actors of his generation, capable of excelling in both theatre and film roles. The cinema, with its ability to make actors' performances immortal, offered McKellen the opportunity to leave an even more lasting mark on the history of acting, and the success of "Richard III" was only the beginning of a film career that was destined to grow ever more in the years that followed.

Ian McKellen's move to film marked a new phase in his career, one characterised by new challenges and opportunities. While theatre remained his first love, film offered him a global stage on which to express his talent. With 'Richard III', McKellen proved that he was able to combine the greatness of Shakespeare's characters with the demands of the film medium, bringing to the screen a performance that would long remain in the memory of audiences and critics alike. His transition from the stage to the big screen was a natural evolution of an extraordinary actor, capable of adapting to any context and of continuing to surprise with his ability to transform himself in every role he played.

Chapter 7. The role of Gandalf

The role of Gandalf in 'The Lord of the Rings' represents one of the most iconic and defining moments in Ian McKellen's career, propelling him to global success and cementing his status as a living legend of cinema. Casting to play the powerful wizard of Middle Earth was a crucial process for director Peter Jackson, who wanted to secure actors who could bring authenticity and gravitas to characters already loved by millions of readers. McKellen, already established as a Shakespearean actor with a solid film career behind him, seemed the perfect choice for the role, although he was not initially the first option. The film's production had considered other leading figures, but once McKellen was chosen, it became evident that no one else could have embodied Gandalf with the same stage presence and emotional intensity. His performance, which would later extend to the three films of The Hobbit trilogy, made the character immortal in popular culture, transforming him into a figure that has drawn generations of fans into the magical worlds created by J.R.R. Tolkien.

McKellen's transformation into Gandalf was both a physical and emotional process. Preparing for the role required considerable effort. McKellen immersed himself completely in the character, studying Tolkien's text in depth to understand the essence of Gandalf, not just as a simple wizard, but as a spiritual and moral guide for all the inhabitants of Middle-earth. Gandalf is more than a wise character: he is a symbol of ancient wisdom, measured power and hope. McKellen understood immediately that Gandalf represented a kind of bridge between worlds: between human rationality and magic, between justice and destructive power. The actor brought all his previous experience of classical theatre, especially his familiarity with Shakespearean characters, and applied that same depth and complexity to the role of Gandalf. The result was a three-dimensional character, capable of alternating moments of great sweetness and lightness with scenes of extraordinary dramatic intensity.

The physical work on the transformation into Gandalf required long days of make-up and costumes. The long beard, pointed hat and cane became the character's hallmarks. But what struck the audience most was McKellen's ability to make believable a thousand-year-old being, endowed with immense powers, yet profoundly human in his gestures and words. Gandalf was a comforting figure for the heroes of the tale, a reassuring presence but also a wise man who carried a burden and ancient knowledge. McKellen succeeded in conveying this duality through acting that was measured but also emotionally charged. When Gandalf admonished Frodo or led the entire

Fellowship of the Ring, the audience felt the actor's charisma and his ability to give depth to every word. The famous 'You shall not pass!' scene, in which Gandalf stands up to the Balrog on the bridge of Khazad-dûm, became instantly iconic thanks to McKellen's vocal and physical power, making that moment one of the most memorable in the film trilogy.

The global success of The Lord of the Rings films transformed Gandalf into one of the most recognisable characters in film history. McKellen, already known for his theatrical performances, became a much-loved figure to international audiences due to the trilogy's global reach. The films, which relied on innovative special effects and epic storytelling, achieved unprecedented popularity, bringing McKellen nominations for major film awards, including the Oscar. However, beyond the official awards, what was most striking was the bond that the audience established with the character of Gandalf. McKellen managed to embody all the positive qualities that Tolkien's fans had always associated with Gandalf: wisdom, courage, humility and a deep sense of duty to goodness. His Gandalf was not just a hero, but a moral guide, capable of giving hope even in the darkest moments. McKellen's ability to make every dialogue meaningful and to bring to life a character who was already a literary icon was one of the keys to the trilogy's success.

The cultural impact of Gandalf, thanks to McKellen's performance, was enormous. The character became a symbol of wisdom and positive power, embodying values of justice, friendship and sacrifice. The audience, especially the younger generation, found in Gandalf a fatherly and protective figure, capable of facing evil without ever losing his humanity. Gandalf's scenes with the young heroes of the Fellowship of the Ring represent one of the trilogy's most emotionally powerful moments, and McKellen was able to imbue these interactions with a gentleness that made his character even more beloved. Moreover, Gandalf's image has continued to live on well beyond the films: the character has become an icon in the world of memes, film quotations, and has left a lasting imprint on popular culture, making McKellen a household name throughout the world, far beyond the theatre circles in which he was already revered.

Part of Gandalf's success is also due to McKellen's ability to work harmoniously with the rest of the cast and director Peter Jackson. The trilogy required tremendous cohesion among the actors and great faith in Jackson's visionary project. McKellen, with his vast experience, was a reference point for many of the young actors who worked on the film, such as Elijah Wood and Orlando Bloom. His professional and generous approach on the set helped to create an atmosphere of great cooperation, and his performance as Gandalf was enriched by this positive atmosphere. Despite the epic scope of the project, McKellen managed to keep the character anchored in a humanity that made him accessible and authentic. In this sense, Gandalf became the moral heart of the trilogy, and McKellen its main spokesman.

The role of Gandalf marked an indelible chapter in Ian McKellen's career, leading him to a global success that few other performances have achieved. Through his performance, the character became a symbol of wisdom and courage that inspired millions of people around the world. McKellen was able to transform a great literary character into a cinematic icon, making his Gandalf unforgettable and strengthening the bond between the audience and the universe created by Tolkien. Gandalf's cultural impact, amplified by the power of the film trilogy, remains one of the greatest testimonies to Ian McKellen's timeless talent.

Chapter 8. The rebirth with 'X-Men' and Magneto

Ian McKellen's participation in the 'X-Men' franchise marked a new phase in his career, confirming his extraordinary ability to adapt to the changes in cinema and to reach an ever-widening audience. If until then he had been recognised as one of the great interpreters of classical theatre and art-house cinema, with the arrival of 'X-Men' in 2000, McKellen approached a genre that seemed distant from his previous roles: superhero films. The world of cinema was undergoing a significant transformation, with the advent of major comic book productions, and Marvel was preparing to launch one of its best-loved sagas, that of the X-Men. Despite his already established theatrical and cinematic success, McKellen seized this opportunity with enthusiasm, once again demonstrating his eclecticism and desire to explore new artistic challenges. The role he was offered was that of Magneto, one of the main antagonists of the mutant world created by Stan Lee and Jack Kirby. This complex and multifaceted character would give McKellen the opportunity to explore a new range of emotions and bring his talents into a context quite different from what he was used to.

Magneto, whose real name is Erik Lehnsherr, is one of the most powerful mutants in the Marvel Universe, gifted with the ability to manipulate magnetic fields and control metals. But beyond his incredible powers, what makes Magneto such a fascinating character is his tragic history and deep-seated motivations. A Holocaust survivor, Erik develops a deep cynicism and a distorted view of reality, convinced that mutants must fight by any means to survive, even at the cost of crushing the humanity that fears and persecutes them. Magneto is the antithesis of Charles Xavier, his old friend and colleague, played by Patrick Stewart, who instead believes in peaceful co-existence between mutants and humans. The rivalry between Magneto and Xavier is one of the pillars of the X-Men saga, and McKellen brought to this relationship an emotional depth that went far beyond the classic opposition between good and evil. In him, Magneto was no mere villain, but a man scarred by pain, trauma and disillusionment. His desire to protect mutants at any cost made him understandable, although his actions were often morally questionable.

McKellen's characterisation of Magneto quickly became a distinctive element of the franchise. His performance added a dimension of humanity and tragedy to the character, making him much more than just a villain. McKellen succeeded in conveying Erik's psychological complexity, oscillating between moments of extreme anger and vengeance, and those of vulnerability, in which the pain of past injustices emerged. His friendship with Xavier, even when the two were on opposite sides, was full of mutual respect and melancholy, making their rivalry more of a philosophical issue than a simple battle between good guys and bad guys. McKellen and Patrick Stewart, both veterans of Shakespearean theatre, brought this dynamism to the big screen, turning a superhero saga into a profound reflection on the nature of hatred, fear and tolerance. Their chemistry was palpable, and the relationship between Magneto and Xavier became one of the most loved and appreciated aspects of the saga, giving the films an emotional weight that was not expected in a genre often associated only with action.

Playing Magneto allowed McKellen to further expand his audience. If until then he had been known mainly to theatre fans and film buffs, with 'X-Men' he managed to reach a much wider audience, including young viewers and comic book fans. The figure of Magneto immediately became iconic, and McKellen succeeded in making the character a symbol of resistance and struggle against oppression, making him a much-loved figure even beyond his moral ambiguity. The film's success not only consolidated the X-Men saga as one of the most important franchises of the 2000s, but helped redefine McKellen's career, proving that an actor of his experience could excel even in unexpected roles and in a genre as popular as superheroes.

The character of Magneto was also an interesting reflection on the nature of power and its consequences. McKellen, with his extraordinary ability to understand the characters he plays, brought a particular nuance to this aspect: Magneto was not simply power-hungry out of selfishness, but firmly believed that domination over mutants was the only way for his race to survive. This viewpoint of his, deeply influenced by the atrocities of the Holocaust, made his worldview bleak but understandable. McKellen portrayed Magneto as a man destroyed by hatred, but who had never entirely lost hope that his old friend Xavier might one day convince him that coexistence between humans and mutants was possible. This tension within the character made his performance particularly fascinating, leading the audience to reflect on the thin line between justice and vengeance, good and evil.

With the role of Magneto, McKellen gained a new generation of fans. Many young viewers who did not know him before his involvement in the X-Men saga were fascinated by his magnetic presence on screen, and began to discover his earlier work as well, recognising in him a rare versatility. Despite the commercial nature of the project, McKellen never treated the role of Magneto as something secondary to his more 'prestigious' work. On the contrary, he approached the character with the same care and attention to detail he had always reserved for more classical roles, making Magneto a complex and tragic figure, capable of generating empathy even at times when his actions seemed indefensible. This dedication led Magneto to become one of the most beloved characters in the saga, so much so that he returned in multiple films in the franchise, with McKellen continuing to explore new facets of the character, making him ever more layered and fascinating.

McKellen's impact as Magneto was not just limited to the X-Men saga. With his performance, he helped elevate the superhero film genre, proving that actors of great depth could also bring added value to commercial projects. His presence gave the films a dignity and prestige that was often lacking in the genre's productions, and paved the way for a new way of conceiving superhero films, in which the depth of the characters and the quality of the performances became key elements for success. Thanks to his Magneto, Ian McKellen was able to demonstrate once again his extraordinary versatility and consolidate his status as a timeless actor, capable of moving from Shakespearean theatre to Hollywood blockbusters with the same passion and dedication.

Chapter 9. Activism for LGBTQ+ rights

Ian McKellen is not only an internationally renowned actor, but also a leading figure in the fight for LGBTQ+ rights, a tireless activist who has put his visibility and prestige at the service of a cause he believes in deeply. His public coming out in 1988 marked a turning point in his personal life and career, but also represented a significant step for the British and international LGBTQ+ community. At the time, being openly gay in show business, and particularly in the conservative theatre and film environment, was still considered a risk. However, McKellen chose to publicly reveal his sexual orientation in response to the infamous 'Section 28', a law introduced by Margaret Thatcher's British government that banned the 'promotion' of homosexuality in schools. For McKellen, the decision to come out was not just a personal act, but a political statement against a law that further stigmatised the already largely marginalised gay and lesbian community. From that moment on, McKellen became one of the most influential and recognisable voices in the civil rights struggle, using his platform to raise awareness and promote equality.

McKellen's commitment to equality and LGBTQ+ rights was not limited to public statements or symbolic appearances. He threw himself into the fight actively, becoming co-founder of Stonewall, a

British organisation that fights for LGBTQ+ rights. Stonewall, founded in the same year as his coming out, quickly became one of the leading civil rights organisations in the UK, and McKellen became its most visible face, using his notoriety to raise awareness of crucial issues such as egalitarian marriage, protection from hate crimes and discrimination in the workplace. His passion for the cause was reflected in every public speech, press conference and campaign he supported. McKellen never treated his activism as an adjunct to his acting career, but rather as central to his life. His visibility as an international star made him a role model for millions of LGBTQ+ people around the world, many of whom found in him a reference point and source of inspiration.

One of the most significant aspects of McKellen's activism was his ability to address complex issues with an empathetic and inclusive approach. He always emphasised the importance of education as a tool to combat homophobia and discrimination, both in schools and in society at large. He never ceased to draw attention to the need for acceptance and respect for diversity, and spoke openly about the impact homophobia had had on his personal and professional life prior to his coming out. In numerous interviews, McKellen reflected on how, for many years, he had hidden his sexuality for fear of prejudice and discrimination, and how liberating it had been to live openly and authentically instead.

This message of authenticity and personal courage became one of the pillars of his advocacy, prompting many other public figures to do the same and contributing to a significant cultural change in the way society perceives homosexuality.

One of his most important battles was for the abolition of 'Section 28', the same law that had prompted him to come out. McKellen worked tirelessly to raise awareness among the public and politicians about the damage this law was causing, particularly to young LGBTQ+ students, who were deprived of the right to feel accepted and represented in schools. The abolition of this law in 2003 was one of the great victories of the British LGBTQ+ movement, and McKellen played a key role in it, not only as an actor but as an activist and leader. This success did not mark the end of his commitment, however. In the years that followed, he continued to champion key community causes, such as the fight for egalitarian marriage, which was finally legalised in the UK in 2014.

International recognition of his activism was not long in coming. McKellen was invited all over the world to speak about LGBTQ+ rights, taking his message even to countries where homosexuality was still criminalised or strongly stigmatised. Although his film career constantly took him around the world, McKellen always found time to attend civil rights events, conferences and rallies, proving that his commitment went far beyond words. He was enthusiastically welcomed at many international Pride events, and his presence at these events was seen as a sign of solidarity and hope for millions of people. His courage in living openly and defending the rights of LGBTQ+ people was recognised with numerous awards and honours, including a knighthood awarded by Queen Elizabeth II in 1991 for his contribution to theatre and, later, the Companion of Honour, one of Britain's highest honours, in 2008, not only for his artistic career but also for his activism.

In addition to being a recognised public figure, McKellen has also worked on a personal level to support young LGBTQ+ actors and to promote greater inclusion in the entertainment industry. He has always spoken about the importance of having positive role models and how film and theatre can play a key role in creating a more inclusive image of society. He never shied away from denouncing discrimination within the film industry, insisting that diversity should be represented not only in front of the camera, but also behind the scenes.

Ian McKellen's legacy as an activist is as important as his legacy as an actor. He has shown that celebrity can be used for noble purposes, to advance crucial battles and give a voice to those who, for too long, have remained silent. His commitment to civil rights and his dedication to the LGBTQ+ cause had a profound impact on a generation of people who found in him a leader, an ally and an example. Through his visibility, courage and perseverance, McKellen has contributed significantly to changing the social and cultural landscape, not only in the UK but worldwide, making the world a little more just and inclusive for LGBTQ+ people.

Chapter 10. Private life and the balance between public and private

Ian McKellen has managed to maintain a delicate balance between his private life and his public career, no mean feat for such a celebrated figure. With a career spanning more than five decades, McKellen has always managed his relationship with the press with intelligence and confidentiality, avoiding letting his private life be overly exposed to the media spotlight. Despite being a world-famous actor, McKellen has managed to maintain a clear distinction between his public persona and his personal existence, carefully protecting his intimate sphere. Unlike many Hollywood stars who see their private lives become the subject of gossip and speculation, McKellen has been able to draw a clear boundary, focusing primarily on his work and using his fame for broader causes, such as LGBTQ+ activism or theatre promotion, rather than feeding the press interest in personal details.

His relationship with the press has always been handled with great care and professionalism. McKellen never shied away from interviews or public events, but managed to maintain a balance between what he was willing to share and what he preferred to keep to himself. This does not mean that he was shy or cold towards the media, quite the contrary. He is known for his humour and affability in public, but it is clear that the focus of his communication has always been his art and civic engagement, rather than his personal life. However, when he felt it was important, he never hesitated to speak openly about aspects of his private life, such as when he came out in 1988 to support the battle against 'Section 28'. That choice, while extremely personal, was made for a political and social reason, demonstrating how McKellen uses his visibility in a thoughtful way, turning moments of his private life into levers to advance social justice battles.

Another interesting aspect of McKellen's private life is his vast circle of friendships in show business. Having worked for decades with some of the most influential figures in theatre and film, McKellen has built lasting relationships with actors, directors and producers from around the world. One of his closest friends is Patrick Stewart, with whom he has shared sets in numerous projects, including the films of the 'X-Men' saga. The relationship between McKellen and Stewart has often been the focus of media attention, not only for their on-screen chemistry, but also for their obvious friendship in real life. The two actors have become icons of a deep and genuine friendship, often appearing together at public events and interviews, displaying genuine affection and mutual respect. This bond offered audiences a rare glimpse into McKellen's private life, highlighting how important genuine human relationships are to him, especially in the often hectic and superficial world of the entertainment industry.

McKellen has also taken on the role of mentor for many young actors, both in theatre and film. As an acting veteran, he has often been called upon to share his experience with new generations of actors, many of whom see him as a reference point and source of inspiration. His ability to move from classical theatre to Hollywood blockbusters with ease, always maintaining a very high quality of interpretation, makes him a rare example of versatility and dedication to the craft. McKellen has never hesitated to offer advice and support to young talent, either through direct collaborations or at public meetings, lectures or master classes. Many young actors have expressed their gratitude for the opportunity to have worked with him and for the support he provided during the early stages of their careers. His role as a mentor was not only professional, but also human: McKellen is known for his generous and humble approach, a trait that has made him particularly loved by his colleagues.

Despite his immense notoriety, McKellen has always maintained a balanced relationship with fame. Unlike many other stars, he never seems to have been obsessed with success or the need to be the centre of attention constantly. For him, acting has always been an art form, a means of exploring the human condition and conveying emotions, rather than a springboard to feed the ego or the desire for stardom. This approach has allowed McKellen to handle his notoriety calmly and without excess, living a relatively quiet private life and devoting himself to what he really loves: theatre, film and his commitment to civil rights. Even at times of increased media exposure, such as after the planetary success of 'Lord of the Rings' and 'X-Men', McKellen has managed to avoid the excesses that often accompany Hollywood fame, preferring to focus on meaningful projects and causes close to his heart.

Managing notoriety has never prevented McKellen from being accessible and approachable to his audience. He is famous for the way he interacts with fans, always showing kindness and gratitude. During numerous public events and appearances at film premieres, McKellen has always shown himself to be affable and open, signing autographs and talking to fans without ever displaying impatience or arrogance. This humility, combined with his extraordinary career, has helped make him not only an icon of film and theatre, but also a beloved figure to audiences around the world. McKellen has managed to maintain his personal and professional integrity even in the most intense spotlight, proving that it is possible to be a star without losing sight of one's humanity and respect for others.

Ian McKellen's private life, although protected and handled confidentially, offers some insights into the man behind the actor. His balance between public and private, his role as mentor and friend, and his ability to handle fame with intelligence and serenity are just some of the aspects that have contributed to making him a unique figure in show business. His life has been characterised by a constant dedication to his art and what he believes in, but also by a deep understanding of the value of human relationships, discretion and the importance of living authentically, both in the public and private spheres.

Chapter 11. Television successes

Ian McKellen's television successes have been an important extension of his already rich and varied career, allowing him to reach new audiences and explore characters that, although in a different format than film and theatre, have allowed him to fully express his versatility as an actor. Despite the fact that his worldwide fame is mainly linked to his major film roles and his Shakespearian theatre performances, McKellen has been able to seize the opportunities offered by the small screen, tackling television projects with the same commitment and dedication that characterise each of his performances. The relationship with television, for McKellen, has always been based on a strong desire to explore new means of expression and to test himself with different stories and formats.

Television, compared to film, often offers actors the opportunity to work on projects that require greater intimacy and prolonged involvement with the audience. This aspect was particularly appreciated by McKellen, who has always loved the direct and almost familiar relationship that television manages to establish with the viewer. Moreover, the serial format, which has become predominant in recent decades, allows actors to delve into their characters over the course of multiple episodes or seasons, giving them the opportunity to explore their evolution and nuances. McKellen has embraced this challenge enthusiastically, participating in series and films for television that have met with great public and critical success.

One of the most notable television projects McKellen has taken part in is the British series 'Vicious', which aired from 2013 to 2016. This sitcom, which saw McKellen starring alongside another giant of British theatre, Derek Jacobi, tells the story of a long-standing gay couple, Freddie and Stuart, who have been living together for more than fifty years and face their old age with irony, sarcasm and hilarious bickering. The series allowed McKellen to demonstrate his extraordinary comic talent, a side that the wider public had had less opportunity to appreciate in his more dramatic film and theatre roles. In 'Vicious', McKellen plays Freddie, a now-retired theatre actor, vain and edgy, who never misses an opportunity to poke his partner with witty and self-deprecating comments. The series was a great success in Britain and gained international notoriety as well, leading McKellen to gain the affection of a new segment of viewers, many of whom may not have been familiar with his more committed theatre or film work.

'Vicious' also represented an important opportunity for the representation of the LGBTQ+ community on television. Although the tone of the series was light and focused on comedy, the fact that the protagonists were an older gay couple helped normalise and celebrate diversity also on the small screen, a theme particularly dear to McKellen. This project, although different from his most iconic roles, once again demonstrated McKellen's ability to take even the lightest projects seriously, making each character multifaceted and unforgettable.

In addition to 'Vicious', McKellen took part in numerous television films that allowed him to express his acting mastery in very different contexts. One of his most memorable roles was that of Bill Condon in the television film 'Mr. Holmes' (2015), where he plays an elderly Sherlock Holmes, now retired, who tries to solve one last mystery before his mind, now weakened by age, betrays him completely. In this film, McKellen brought to life a character who perfectly embodies the theme of old age, physical and mental decline, and the struggle to keep one's dignity intact. His portrayal of Sherlock Holmes was praised for its delicacy and emotional depth, once again confirming his ability to bring new nuances to iconic characters.

McKellen's relationship with the small screen demonstrated how, although theatre and film have always been his primary mediums, television has offered a different and interesting context for exploring more intimate roles and characters closer to the everyday. McKellen has been able to exploit the versatility of television to reach different audiences and expand his sphere of influence as an actor. This has not only allowed him to further consolidate his prestige, but also to build a closer bond with audiences, who often find television a more accessible and familiar means of entertainment. Although film remains McKellen's main source of fame, television has allowed him to tackle projects that, in some ways, complement his artistic journey. Each television role seems to have been carefully chosen, in line with his passion for stories that deal with major human themes, such as friendship, old age, pride, memory and identity. Even in a television context, where the risk of trivialisation can be higher than in film or theatre projects, McKellen has never allowed his characters to lose complexity or depth. This is perhaps one of the aspects that distinguishes him most: his ability to make each role shine, regardless of the medium through which it is brought to the public.

The impact of television on McKellen's career is also reflected in his ability to adapt to changes in the entertainment industry. With the rise of streaming platforms and the increasing success of television series over traditional films, McKellen has shown an ability to reinvent himself, continuing to be relevant and appreciated even in an ever-changing media landscape. His move to television was not a fallback, but a conscious choice to explore new territory and reach new heights in his extraordinary career.

Ian McKellen's television successes testify to his ability to tackle any role, regardless of format, with the same intensity and dedication that have made him one of the world's best-loved and most respected actors. His versatility, combined with his passion for the art of acting, has allowed him to make his mark on the small screen as well, building a television career that has expanded his audience and consolidated his reputation as a complete and timeless actor.

Chapter 12. The return to theatre

The call of the stage has always been a constant in Ian McKellen's life. Despite his international film successes, with iconic roles in films such as 'Lord of the Rings' and 'X-Men', McKellen has never left the theatre, his true artistic home. McKellen's bond with the theatre is rooted in a deep passion for the art of live acting and for direct contact with the audience. For him, the stage represents a sacred place, where actor and spectator share an immediate and authentic experience that film and television, fascinating as they are, cannot replicate in the same way. The theatre allows McKellen to explore the characters in depth, night after night, in a continuous process of discovery and refinement. Each performance is unique, influenced by the energy of the audience and the feeling of the moment, and this dynamic aspect is what has always drawn him back to the stage, even when his film career was at its peak.

In recent decades, despite his constant commitment to film, McKellen has continued to devote himself to the theatre with projects that reflect his inexhaustible desire to act and his ability to reinvent himself. One of the most significant roles in his recent return to the stage was that of King Lear, in the 2017 production at the Chichester Festival Theatre, later transferred to London's West End. This role, one of the most challenging and complex in Shakespeare's repertoire, was both a challenge and a return to his roots for McKellen. King Lear is a tragic and monumental character, requiring an artistic maturity and emotional depth that few actors can sustain. McKellen, now in the full maturity of his career, tackled the role with the same intensity and passion he had in his early years on stage, once again demonstrating his ability to transform himself and explore new aspects of acting even in roles he has known all his life.

His portrayal of King Lear was acclaimed by critics and audiences alike, not only for its dramatic power, but also for the vulnerability and fragility that McKellen was able to instil in the character. His Lear is a man confronted with his mortality, loss of power and loneliness, themes that resonate deeply with the universal human experience. McKellen was able to make the character accessible and touching, going beyond the grandeur of the Shakespearean text and delivering an intimate and nuanced performance. This type of role, which requires a deep connection with the audience, is exactly what drives McKellen to return to the theatre again and again: the need to challenge himself, to live an artistic experience that puts him in direct contact with the spectator, without filters.

McKellen's relationship with the live audience has always been one of the most fascinating aspects of his theatre work. His stage presence, combined with an extraordinary capacity for empathy, allows him to establish an immediate bond with the viewer. Unlike cinema, where the performance is mediated by the camera and editing, theatre offers McKellen the opportunity to live and share the moment with the audience in a pure and direct way. This exchange of energy between actor and spectator is something that McKellen has always considered fundamental to his work, and which drives him to return to the stage despite his film commitments. For him, each evening is a new opportunity to explore the character and to discover something new about himself as an actor, thanks to the reaction of the audience.

Another important aspect of McKellen's return to the theatre is his continued efforts to maintain a balance between film and stage. Despite the planetary success of his film roles, McKellen has always found a way to return to the theatre while maintaining a disciplined and rigorous approach to live acting. This balance between the two worlds is the secret of his artistic longevity: on the one hand, film has given him the opportunity to reach a global audience and play roles with great visual and narrative impact; on the other, theatre has offered him the chance to continue exploring acting in a more personal and profound way, without the limitations imposed by film productions. McKellen is one of the few actors of his generation who has managed to maintain this duality, avoiding being caged in one medium and continuing to grow artistically.

Theatre has also allowed McKellen to experiment more freely with form and content. In recent years, he has participated in a number of smaller, independent theatre projects that have given him the opportunity to work in less structured and more creative contexts than the big blockbuster films. These projects, often performed in smaller theatres or during festivals, have shown a side of McKellen that many audiences did not know: an actor who is not afraid to take risks and put himself on the line in less conventional roles and productions. These projects allowed him to keep his artistic curiosity alive and explore new horizons, both technically and emotionally.

In addition, returning to the theatre offered McKellen the opportunity to contribute to the training of a new generation of actors. Thanks to his vast experience and dedication to his craft, McKellen has often taken on the role of mentor for young actors who have had the opportunity to work with him. On stage, McKellen is a charismatic and generous presence, offering advice and support to his younger colleagues, helping them to grow artistically and develop their skills. This spirit of collaboration is one of the aspects that makes the theatre such an important part of his career, and one that drives him to return whenever he can.

Ian McKellen's return to the theatre represents an essential chapter in his career, an irresistible lure that has led him to continue exploring the boundaries of acting and cultivating his love for the stage. The direct relationship with the audience, the opportunity to work on classic and contemporary texts, and the constant challenge that theatre represents for an actor of his stature, are all elements that explain why McKellen can never completely abandon the theatre. It is there, on those wooden boards, that he began his artistic journey, and it is there that he continues to find his most authentic creative expression.

Chapter 13. Memorable collaborations

Ian McKellen's memorable collaborations have helped shape not only his career, but also the international film and theatre landscape. One of the aspects that have made him such a beloved and respected figure is his ability to create a special chemistry with the actors and directors he has worked with, building artistic and personal bonds that have led to extraordinary results both on stage and screen. These relationships, based on mutual esteem and a deep passion for the art of acting, have allowed McKellen to tackle iconic roles and explore new creative horizons, always driven by collaboration with some of the film and theatre industry's brightest minds.

One of the most significant collaborations of McKellen's career has been with colleague and friend Patrick Stewart. The two actors, both British theatre veterans and film legends, have shared the stage on numerous occasions, but their closest bond was cemented through the 'X-Men' movie saga. McKellen plays Magneto, the series' iconic antagonist, while Stewart is his friend and rival, Professor Charles Xavier. On set, the chemistry between the two was evident from the start, leading to a series of powerful and memorable scenes that greatly enhanced the emotional depth of the film. Their on-screen rivalry, characterised by a constant duel of intelligence and power, was made even more intense by the strong personal bond that exists between the two actors in real life. Beyond the film franchise, McKellen and Stewart have also taken their friendship to the theatrical stage, performing together in such classic plays as 'Waiting for Godot' and 'No Man's Land'. These critically acclaimed shows showcased the extraordinary chemistry between the two, with performances that oscillated between the comic and the tragic, reflecting their ability to elevate the material with their impeccable acting and deep mutual respect.

But the collaboration with Stewart is just one of many in McKellen's long career. Over the years, he has had the privilege of working with some of the most talented and innovative directors in the industry, including Peter Jackson, who directed McKellen in 'The Lord of the Rings' trilogy and later in 'The Hobbit'. The role of Gandalf, played by McKellen, has become one of the most iconic in film history, and much of the credit goes to Jackson's extraordinary vision and his ability to bring out the best in his actors. McKellen has always spoken with great admiration of his work with Jackson, describing him as a visionary director who knew how to build a complex and engaging cinematic world while giving actors the space they needed to explore their characters in a deep and personal way. This collaboration had a huge impact not only on McKellen's career, but also on contemporary cinema, taking the fantasy genre to a new level of artistic and narrative excellence.

Another major collaboration in McKellen's career was with director Bill Condon, who directed him in two highly acclaimed films: 'Demons and Gods' (1998) and 'Mr. Holmes' (2015). In 'Demons and Gods', McKellen played director James Whale, known for directing the horror classics 'Frankenstein' and 'The Bride of Frankenstein'. The film explores the last days of Whale's life and his struggle with inner demons related to his past and his sexuality. McKellen's performance was praised for its intensity and vulnerability, and led to the actor earning his first Oscar nomination. Condon, a sensitive and careful director, was able to create an environment in which McKellen could explore the more complex and darker sides of the character, allowing him to deliver one of the most moving performances of his career. Also in 'Mr. Holmes', Condon entrusted McKellen with the role of a popular culture icon, Sherlock Holmes, now elderly and struggling with memory loss. Once again, the collaboration between director and actor produced an intimate and fascinating portrait of a man grappling with decline and his own legacy.

McKellen's artistic friendships are not only limited to directors and actors with whom he has worked directly, but also extend to figures who have inspired and influenced him throughout his career. Over the years, he has always cited Laurence

Olivier as one of his greatest inspirations. Olivier, with his extraordinary ability to switch from theatre to film with ease and mastery, was a model of versatility and artistic commitment for McKellen. Although the two never collaborated in any significant way, Olivier's influence on McKellen was palpable, especially in his early years in theatre, when he tackled Shakespearean roles with the same intensity and passion that he saw in Olivier's work.

McKellen's collaborations have had a lasting impact not only on his career, but also on those who have worked alongside him. His generosity as an actor, his willingness to share the stage and screen without ever wanting to dominate the scene, made him an ideal partner for many colleagues, who always praised his professionalism and commitment. Young and veteran actors have found in him a mentor and a friend, a figure capable of elevating the collective work with his presence and experience. His ability to create authentic bonds with his colleagues made every collaboration an opportunity for growth, not only for him, but for all those who had the privilege of working alongside him.

Every director, actor or crew member who has worked with him has had the opportunity to experience not only his extraordinary talent, but also his humility and his desire to create something meaningful through art. These bonds, spanning decades of his career, have produced some of the most memorable performances in film and theatre history, and have helped make McKellen not only a legendary actor, but also a central figure in the international arts community.

Chapter 14. Dedication to social causes

Ian McKellen is known not only for his extraordinary artistic career, but also for his unwavering dedication to social causes, particularly for the LGBTQ+ community and the fight against discrimination. From the moment he decided to come out publicly in 1988, McKellen has become one of the most influential and influential voices in the civil rights movement, using his celebrity and platform to advocate crucial battles and inspire change in a world still marked by prejudice and injustice. His commitment has never been limited to empty words or token appearances: McKellen has devoted time and concrete energy to advancing his convictions, combining his passion for acting with an ethical vision that has always focused on dignity and respect for every human being.

Her coming out was a defining moment, not only for her personal life, but also for the entire LGBTQ+ community. In 1988, at the height of the debate on the infamous 'Section 28' - a British law that prohibited the promotion of homosexuality in schools and public bodies - McKellen decided to publicly reveal his homosexuality, realising that remaining silent was no longer an option. This law, perceived by many as an act of repression and discrimination against LGBTQ+ people, prompted McKellen to come forward and use his position to openly oppose these unjust policies. Since then, his activism has become an integral part of his public identity, turning him into a champion for civil rights and a figurehead for many generations.

Over the years, McKellen has continued to fight tirelessly for equality and against discrimination of all kinds. He was a founding member of Stonewall, one of the UK's leading LGBTQ+ rights organisations, which played a crucial role in promoting legislative changes for equality, including the legalisation of same-sex marriage and the fight for equal rights in the workplace. McKellen's presence within this organisation has given enormous visibility to the battles waged by Stonewall, helping to raise awareness and break the silence on issues that had been considered taboo for too long. His contribution was never limited to the UK: McKellen attended events and conferences all over the world, promoting a culture of respect and inclusion wherever he was.

One of the most admirable aspects of his commitment is his ability to link his passion for activism with his artistic work. For McKellen, art and politics have never been two separate worlds: he deeply believes that theatre, film and television can be powerful tools to educate, raise awareness and promote social change. He has always tried to choose roles that reflect his worldview, favouring stories that speak of justice, equality and human rights. In each of his performances, whether historical characters or fictional figures, McKellen brought with him a deep awareness of the real struggles that many people face every day, giving his performances a human and universal dimension that transcends mere entertainment.

In addition to his work for the LGBTQ+ community, McKellen has always spoken out against all forms of discrimination, whether based on sexual orientation, gender, ethnicity or socio-economic status. He has strongly advocated the need to create a more equal and inclusive society, in which everyone has the same opportunities to express themselves and live a full and dignified life. His commitment against racism and xenophobia has been equally determined: McKellen has participated in numerous campaigns in favour of migrants' rights and against exclusionary policies, emphasising the importance of welcoming and respecting cultural diversity. For him, diversity is an asset and not a threat, and this conviction has always guided his approach both personally and professionally.

Supporting humanitarian organisations is another key chapter in McKellen's life. In addition to Stonewall, he has worked with numerous NGOs working in the fields of human rights, health and education, both in the UK and internationally. He has supported Amnesty International's campaign against torture and unlawful detention, and lent his voice to raise awareness of the living conditions of refugees and those displaced by war and conflict.

In addition, McKellen has always shown a strong commitment to environmental issues, participating in initiatives to raise awareness about climate change and promote a more sustainable lifestyle. He has supported various Greenpeace campaigns and has repeatedly stressed the importance of taking concrete action to preserve the planet for future generations.

His commitment is deeply rooted in an ethical worldview, based on the fundamental principle of equality and respect for all human beings. For McKellen, the privilege of being a celebrity has never been an end in itself, but a tool to make a difference in the world. This sense of social responsibility is what distinguishes him as a public figure and as an activist. His ability to remain true to his values, even when facing criticism or pressure, has inspired millions of people around the world, proving that change is possible when one acts with courage and conviction.

His influence extends far beyond the stage and screen: he is a moral leader, a living example of how civic engagement can be an integral part of a successful artistic and public life. For McKellen, change happens not only through big actions, but also through small everyday gestures, through the way we relate to others and choose to treat those around us. This philosophy of life, which focuses on dignity and respect for the individual, is what has made McKellen not only one of the most respected actors in the world, but also a figure of hope and inspiration for anyone striving for a more just and inclusive world.

Ian McKellen's dedication to social causes is one of the most significant aspects of his life and career. The actor has been able to turn his celebrity into an instrument of change, using his voice and position to support fundamental battles for civil and human rights. With his tireless commitment and ethical worldview, McKellen has shown that art and activism can go hand in hand, helping to build a fairer, more just and more humane society.

Chapter 15. Ian McKellen and the Royal Shakespeare Company

Ian McKellen has maintained a deep and enduring connection with the Royal Shakespeare Company (RSC), one of the world's most prestigious theatrical institutions, and his relationship with this company has significantly defined his career as a Shakespearean actor. From the very beginning, theatre has been a place of discovery and authentic artistic expression for McKellen, and the RSC, with its extraordinary repertoire of classic plays, particularly by William Shakespeare, has offered the actor a stage on which to consolidate his professional identity. Over the years, McKellen has become an iconic figure in British theatre, giving legendary performances that have enriched and transformed the way Shakespeare's plays are perceived by modern audiences.

His joining the Royal Shakespeare Company in the 1970s marked the beginning of one of the most important collaborations of his professional life. The RSC represented a unique opportunity for McKellen to work closely with some of the greatest actors and directors on the British theatre scene, challenging him with some of the most complex and demanding roles in Shakespeare's repertoire. Thanks to the discipline and rigour demanded by the RSC, McKellen was able to hone his acting technique, developing a meticulous and intense approach that has become one of his defining characteristics. His early roles within the company allowed him to build a reputation as one of the most promising performers of his generation, and he was soon recognised as one of the leading Shakespearean actors of his time.

One of the roles that marked McKellen's career with the RSC was that of Macbeth, one of Shakespeare's darkest and most powerful tragedies. His portrayal of the tormented Scottish king is still remembered as one of the most intense and memorable ever. McKellen managed to capture the psychological complexity of the character, exploring his gradual descent into madness and despair with an emotional depth that left audiences spellbound. His performance in 'Macbeth' demonstrated his extraordinary ability to fully immerse himself in the characters, turning each scene into an emotional and psychological journey. Alongside Judi Dench, who played Lady Macbeth, McKellen created one of the most powerful couples ever seen on stage, making the production an unprecedented success and a landmark for lovers of Shakespearean theatre.

Another iconic role McKellen brought to the RSC was that of Richard III, one of the most famous 'villains' in theatrical history. His portrayal of Richard III was praised for its brilliant combination of cruelty and charm, leading audiences to sympathise, albeit reluctantly, with such a manipulative and ruthless character. McKellen managed to make Richard's moral complexity palpable, balancing his ruthless ambition with a dark charisma that made him irresistible. The production had such an impact that McKellen turned his stage role into a 1995 film, set in an alternative fascist era, once again demonstrating his ability to bring Shakespeare's classics to new audiences, renewing their power and relevance.

But McKellen's contribution to the RSC is not limited to these legendary roles. The actor has played many other Shakespearean characters, including Hamlet, Coriolanus and King Lear, in a career that has seen him explore the different nuances of the human soul through Shakespeare's immortal words. Each role has been an opportunity for McKellen to deepen his understanding of human nature, using Shakespeare's powerful and poetic language as a vehicle to express universal emotions and conflicts. His evolution as a Shakespearean actor has been a constant search for truth and authenticity, and McKellen has always tried to make his characters accessible and understandable to contemporary audiences, proving that the themes Shakespeare deals with - ambition, love, jealousy, power and madness - are eternal and speak to all generations. McKellen's connection with the Royal Shakespeare Company has contributed significantly to British culture, not only through his extraordinary artistic contribution, but also because of the way he has helped spread Shakespeare's work internationally. Through his performances, McKellen has become an ambassador of British culture, taking Shakespeare's plays around the world and showing how vibrant and contemporary classical theatre can be. His contribution to the RSC has also inspired a new generation of actors, many of whom see McKellen as a mentor and role model. His dedication to his craft, his tireless pursuit of perfection and his love of theatre have made him a respected and admired figure not only by his colleagues, but also by critics and spectators.

Another crucial aspect of McKellen's work with the RSC has been his commitment to making theatre accessible to a wider audience. Through touring, television productions and film adaptations, he has helped take Shakespeare outside the traditional confines of the theatre, reaching people who otherwise would not have had the opportunity to see these plays live. His belief that theatre should be an art that is accessible to all, not just a cultural elite, has guided many of his professional choices, and McKellen has always tried to find innovative ways to engage audiences and make theatre a vital part of modern cultural life.

Over the years, McKellen's relationship with the RSC has become one of the most fruitful and inspiring collaborations of his career, a partnership that has led to performances that have gone down in British theatre history. His contribution to the evolution of the Shakespearean actor is undeniable: McKellen has shown that an actor can continually reinvent himself, bringing new nuances and depth to the characters he plays, even after decades of his career. His commitment to classical theatre, combined with his extraordinary ability to turn each role into a unique and unforgettable experience, has cemented his status as one of the greatest Shakespearean actors of all time.

The Royal Shakespeare Company has been more than just a workplace for Ian McKellen: it has been the cradle of his artistic evolution, a creative refuge where he has been able to explore the boundaries of theatre and acting. The bond between McKellen and the RSC continues to be a fundamental part of his artistic identity, a relationship that has enriched not only his career but also the history of British theatre. His contribution to Shakespeare's legacy is incalculable, and his commitment to keeping Shakespeare's work alive and relevant makes him a key figure in world theatre culture.

Chapter 16. His impact on fantasy cinema

Ian McKellen's impact on fantasy cinema is undeniable, and his iconic roles as Gandalf in the 'Lord of the Rings' trilogy and Magneto in the 'X-Men' saga have had a profound and lasting influence not only on his career, but on the entire genre. These characters cemented his reputation as one of the most versatile and charismatic actors of his generation, proving that even in the context of fantasy worlds and epic narratives, acting can reach levels of emotional depth and complexity that speak to audiences of all ages and backgrounds. Fantasy cinema, often considered a secondary genre compared to drama or comedy, has found in McKellen a performer capable of giving dignity and human breath to its protagonists, making stories of magic, superpowers and mythological creatures universal and touching.

The role of Gandalf is perhaps the one that brought Ian McKellen unprecedented worldwide fame. When Peter Jackson began work on the ambitious Lord of the Rings trilogy based on J.R.R. Tolkien's novels, it was clear from the start that Gandalf, the wise and powerful sorcerer, would be one of the saga's key characters. McKellen, already known for his theatre career and his work in dramatic films, was chosen to play Gandalf and immediately became synonymous with the character. His performance combined profound wisdom with a touch of humanity that made the character beloved not only by fans of Tolkien's books, but also by a new generation of viewers encountering the world of Middle-earth for the first time. Gandalf, with his pointed hat, staff and long white beard, could easily have fallen into the stereotype of the 'traditional wizard', but McKellen succeeded in making the character complex and three-dimensional, an immortal being who cares for his friends and the world around him with a deep sense of responsibility and affection. His authority as a spiritual guide and military leader was always balanced by moments of great humanity, such as his affection for the little hobbits or his unshakable faith in goodness, even in the most desperate situations. One of the most important aspects of his role as Gandalf was the impact the character had on young viewers. Gandalf has become a symbol of wisdom, courage and hope for many generations, and McKellen's performance has helped make these values universal and accessible to all. At a time when fantasy cinema was beginning to gain greater recognition and an ever wider audience, McKellen played a key role in demonstrating that films in this genre could offer more than just adventure or spectacular special effects. With his Gandalf, he gave emotional depth and intellectual depth to a figure that might have remained two-dimensional, making him a benchmark not only for the saga, but for all fantasy cinema. Many young viewers found in

Gandalf a hero different from the usual protagonists: not a young warrior or a brave adventurer, but a wise mentor who fights with intelligence and heart, rather than brute force. Similarly, Magneto's role in the 'X-Men' saga represented a unique opportunity for McKellen to explore another complex and layered character within the fantasy genre. Magneto, the X-Men's antagonist, is not the stereotypical 'villain': he is a man with a traumatic past, a Holocaust survivor, who tries to protect mutants - human beings with special powers - from the discrimination and persecution they suffer. McKellen brought to this role a gravitas rare in superhero films, making Magneto a tragic character, driven not by inherent evil, but by the belief that violence is the only way to ensure the survival of his species. His rivalry with Professor Charles Xavier, played by Patrick Stewart, is one of the central elements of the saga, and their interactions are often charged with an emotional tension that transcends the simple conflict between good and evil. Magneto, like Gandalf, is a character that McKellen has played with great psychological depth, exploring the moral dilemmas and ambiguities that define him.

The importance of these fantasy roles in McKellen's career cannot be underestimated. Although he already had a solid theatre and film career behind him, these films allowed him to reach a global audience, turning him into a true cultural icon. In a film industry increasingly dominated by franchises and blockbusters, McKellen managed to elevate his characters far beyond mere entertainment, bringing a depth and dignity that helped redefine what fantasy cinema can offer. This has also had a significant impact on the perception of films in this genre by critics and audiences. Fantasy films, often considered second-rate compared to dramas, have gained a new respectability thanks to performances like McKellen's, proving that it is possible to tell epic and engaging stories without sacrificing emotional and intellectual complexity.

The cultural legacy of the characters Gandalf and Magneto is deep and enduring. These characters have become symbols for several generations of viewers, inspiring not only those who have followed their adventures on screen, but also those who have found in them role models and role models. Gandalf represents wisdom, goodness and perseverance, a character who embodies universal values and has inspired millions to believe in the power of goodness. Magneto, on the other hand, offers a more complex perspective on justice and the fight for rights, showing how trauma and injustice suffered can shape the way a person sees the world. Both characters, thanks to McKellen's extraordinary performance, will continue to influence popular culture for years to come, and their impact will not be forgotten.

Ian McKellen's influence on fantasy cinema is immense. With his portrayals of Gandalf and Magneto, he redefined what it means to be a hero and antagonist within a genre often relegated to simpler, more linear roles. He gave depth and complexity to iconic characters, leaving a cultural legacy that will continue to inspire actors, directors and audiences for many generations. His ability to bring fantasy worlds alive and believable has helped elevate the fantasy genre, proving that stories of magic and superpowers can have as much emotional and intellectual impact as any human drama.

Chapter 17. The evolution of the mature actor

Ian McKellen's artistic evolution after the age of 50 represents one of the most fascinating and significant chapters of his career. If the first half of his professional life was characterised by classic roles in the theatre and powerful, rigorous performances on the big screen, maturity brought with it a new phase of growth and discovery, in which McKellen was able to reinvent himself and adapt to the changes in the world of entertainment, tackling roles that not only enhanced his experience, but also offered audiences a deeper, more multifaceted image of him as an actor. After the age of 50, McKellen explored new artistic territories, playing characters that reflected his age and wisdom, demonstrating surprising versatility and the ability to turn each stage of his career into an opportunity to grow and challenge himself further.

One of the most remarkable aspects of McKellen's mature career has been his ability to balance highly successful commercial roles, such as Gandalf in 'Lord of the Rings' or Magneto in the 'X-Men' saga, with more intimate, theatrical projects that emphasised his deep connection with the characters and the text. It is not easy for an actor to stay relevant and continue to challenge himself in an industry that often tends to favour youth, but McKellen has managed to find the perfect balance between big-name blockbusters and dramatic roles that have allowed him to fully express his craft. In films like 'Mr. Holmes', for example, McKellen showed a new sensibility, playing an elderly Sherlock Holmes, fatigued by time and memory loss, but still endowed with the intellectual brilliance that made him legendary. In this role, McKellen infused a touching vulnerability, exploring the limits and frailties of age with an intensity that touched the audience deeply. This ability to reflect on the passage of time, inevitable physical decline and loss of power, without ever losing his trademark dignity and acumen, marked a crucial evolution in his artistic career.

Maturity has also allowed McKellen to further deepen his relationship with time and experience, both as an actor and as a man. If in his early career energy and physical strength were at the core of his performances, as time went on, McKellen learned to rely on a more subtle and complex range of emotions and nuances. His acting became more meditative, less tied to physical performance and more focused on the psychology and emotionality of the characters. This evolution was not just a response to natural ageing, but a conscious choice to embrace the experience accumulated over the years and use it to enrich his characters with a depth that only time and lived life can give. In this sense, McKellen has demonstrated an extraordinary ability to adapt, avoiding becoming entrenched in stereotypical roles or repeating himself, and instead approaching each new project with a sense of freshness and personal challenge.

Another central aspect of McKellen's artistic growth has been his ability to continually reinvent himself. In an industry where it is easy to be labelled and relegated to certain types of roles, McKellen has always tried to escape these categorisations, exploring a wide range of genres and characters. From Shakespearean theatre to superhero movies, historical dramas and comedies, McKellen has proved that there is no defined boundary to his talent. His versatility has been a key factor in his success in the latter part of his career: he has never been afraid to take on unusual or risky roles, proving that, even after decades of experience, it is possible to continue to surprise and fascinate audiences. This willingness to reinvent himself is reflected not only in his choice of roles, but also in his interpretation of them. McKellen has always tried to approach each character as if for the first time, bringing a meticulous attention to detail and a deep empathy for the conflicts and dilemmas of his protagonists.

McKellen's relationship with time and experience is also evident in the way he has been able to become a mentor for younger actors. His maturity has not been limited to an individual development, but has become an asset to the entertainment world as a whole. McKellen has always shown great willingness to share his knowledge and experience with younger colleagues, offering advice and support to anyone who asks. His role as a mentor was not only a matter of passing on acting techniques, but also of moral and ethical inspiration. McKellen always emphasised the importance of remaining true to oneself and pursuing one's artistic path with honesty and integrity, regardless of industry pressures or external expectations. This approach has influenced many young actors, who see him not only as a master of the stage, but also as a role model of consistency and commitment to the art.

Another element that characterised McKellen's evolution as a mature actor was his growing awareness of the power and responsibility that comes with being a public figure. Over the years, McKellen has used his fame not only to promote his artistic projects, but also to support causes close to his heart, such as LGBTQ+ rights and the fight against discrimination. His maturity has led him to realise that celebrity is not an end in itself, but a tool that can be used to make a difference in the world. This sense of responsibility has become an integral part of his public identity, and his activism has gone hand in hand with his artistic growth, proving that the evolution of an actor is not only about perfecting his technical skills, but also about broadening his worldview and his commitment to others.

Ian McKellen's evolution as a mature actor has been a path of continuous growth, in which the accumulated experience has enriched not only his performances, but also his way of seeing and living life. The ability to adapt to the passage of time, to constantly reinvent himself and to embrace the wisdom that comes with age has made McKellen a unique actor on the international scene, capable of tackling complex and challenging roles with a depth and sensitivity that only a mature artist can achieve. His journey proves that an actor's career is not defined by youth or physical strength, but by the ability to grow, evolve and continue to seek new artistic challenges, with the same passion and dedication that has always characterised his work.

Chapter 18. Awards and acknowledgements

Throughout his long career, Ian McKellen has received numerous prizes and awards that testify not only to his extraordinary talent as an actor, but also to his indelible impact in the world of theatre and film. These awards are not just trophies, but are a symbol of the respect and admiration that the industry, critics and audiences have for him. McKellen has always approached each role with dedication, seriousness and a deep understanding of the characters he plays, and this has led to a series of performances that will go down in history. Among the most important recognitions are the nominations and awards he has received at the most prestigious film and theatre events, such as the Oscars, BAFTAs, Golden Globes and many others, which have celebrated his artistic contribution and his unwavering commitment to the pursuit of excellence.

One of his first major victories came in 1981 with the Tony Award for his portrayal of Antonio in 'Bent', a play dealing with the persecution of homosexuals during the Holocaust. This award marked a pivotal moment in McKellen's career, demonstrating his ability to tackle difficult topics with emotional depth and extraordinary sensitivity. His performance in 'Bent' not only earned him one of the most prestigious awards in theatre, but also cemented his reputation as one of the most versatile and courageous actors of his generation, capable of playing roles that deeply touch the viewer and provoke reflection.

In the film world, McKellen has received several nominations for Academy Awards, the Oscars, one of the highest honours in the field of acting. His first Oscar nomination came in 1999 for his role in 'Demons and Gods', where he played director James Whale, known for the classic films 'Frankenstein' and 'The Bride of Frankenstein'. The role of Whale, who dealt with his sexuality and inner demons in the last days of his life, allowed McKellen to explore a complex and tormented character with emotional finesse. This performance earned him a nomination for Best Actor in a Leading Role, bringing his name to the attention of a wider audience, as well as international critics. Although he did not win an Oscar, the nomination represented an important recognition of his acting mastery and his ability to bring deeply human characters to life.

Another performance that earned him an Oscar nomination was Gandalf in 'The Lord of the Rings: The Fellowship of the Ring' in 2002, where he was nominated for Best Supporting Actor. This iconic role soon became synonymous with McKellen himself, bringing the character of Gandalf to be loved by generations of fans around the world. His ability to combine wisdom, humour and deep empathy made Gandalf one of the most memorable characters in film history, and the Oscar nomination was a well-deserved endorsement of his extraordinary work. Although he did not win the statuette, the nomination reinforced his reputation as one of the most important actors in contemporary cinema.

McKellen has also received numerous BAFTAs (British Academy of Film and Television Arts) throughout his career. In 1997, he was awarded the BAFTA for Best Actor for 'Rasputin', a television film in which he played the Russian mystic who had a great influence on the Russian royal family. This award once again underlined his versatility, proving that McKellen was able to excel not only on the big screen, but also in high-quality television productions. In 2006, he received the BAFTA Fellowship, an honour that is only awarded to personalities who have made an outstanding contribution to the world of film, television or media. This award was a recognition of McKellen's career, celebrating not only his outstanding performances, but also his unwavering commitment to theatre and the British film industry.

The Golden Globes are another important recognition in McKellen's career. In 1997, he won the Golden Globe for Best Supporting Actor for his performance in 'Rasputin'. His performance, intense and charismatic, was praised for its ability to capture the complexity and enigmatic nature of such a controversial historical figure. This award was further confirmation of his talent in transforming complex and contradictory figures, giving them a new life on screen.

Besides the official awards, one of the most significant aspects of McKellen's career has been the gratitude and affection of the public. Many of the characters he has played, from Gandalf to Magneto, have become icons of popular culture, and his ability to connect with viewers has led millions to recognise him as one of the most beloved figures in contemporary cinema. Fans around the world have always seen him as a familiar presence, a figure who conveys wisdom and humanity, both through his roles and his public persona. His kindness and availability to fans, together with his passion for theatre and film, have made him not only a respected actor, but also a true living legend.

Despite all the awards and accolades he has received, McKellen has always maintained a humble approach to his work, recognising that acting is a collective art form and that each award reflects the contribution of many people, from directors to screenwriters to fellow actors. He has often emphasised the importance of collaboration in the creative process, recalling that behind every great performance is a whole team of people working passionately to bring a meaningful story to life.

From the Oscars to the BAFTAs, from the Golden Globes to the Tony Awards, each award has celebrated a different aspect of his art, emphasising his versatility, his commitment and his ability to touch the hearts of viewers. However, perhaps the greatest accolade is the affection and gratitude of the audience, who have found in McKellen not only a great actor, but also an example of integrity, commitment and passion for the art of acting.

Chapter 19. Ian McKellen and independent cinema

Ian McKellen has always shown a deep love for independent cinema, an area in which he has been able to explore a wide range of low-budget projects that have given him the opportunity to express his art without the limitations imposed by large studios. For McKellen, independent cinema represents a space of creative freedom where stories can be told with greater authenticity, where experimentation is encouraged and bold choices are not only allowed, but are often the beating heart of the project. This passion for research cinema has led him to choose roles and collaborations that many actors of his fame might have avoided, embracing instead the risk and uncertainty that often accompany independent projects. His career has been marked by a constant commitment to young directors and new talent, to whom he has offered not only his support, but also his experience and prestige.

One of the aspects that characterises McKellen's work in independent cinema is his willingness to tackle complex themes and deeply human characters, often reflecting moral or existential dilemmas. Mainstream cinema, while having its value and offering great opportunities for visibility, often limits the depth of characters in favour of simpler or more accessible narratives. Independent cinema, on the other hand, is for

McKellen a fertile ground in which to explore human nature in all its complexity. It is here that he has been able to bring to life performances that, although they have not always received the attention of the general public, have enriched his career and demonstrated his commitment to the art of acting. For him, each independent project is an opportunity to challenge himself, to try his hand at roles that require an intimate and psychologically profound approach.

One of McKellen's best known independent films is 'Demons and Gods', a low-budget project that allowed him to explore a complex and tormented character. The film chronicles the life of James Whale, a cult director known for his horror classics such as 'Frankenstein' and 'The Bride of Frankenstein', and his struggle with isolation and depression in the last years of his life. Whale, openly homosexual at a time when this entailed enormous risks for his career and private life, becomes a character in which McKellen was able to explore the theme of loneliness, decline and social repression. The film, shot on a shoestring budget, allowed McKellen to give one of his most moving and intimate performances, earning him his first Oscar nomination. 'Demons and Gods' is a perfect example of how independent cinema can offer stories that go beyond genre conventions, allowing actors to explore unconventional roles with a freedom that is often lacking in big blockbusters.

The choice to work on independent projects was never, for McKellen, dictated by the need to keep his career afloat or to find opportunities in a difficult market, but rather by a deep desire to contribute to stories that he felt were important. He has always recognised the intrinsic value of independent cinema as a place where new ideas can be born and flourish, and where young filmmakers can experiment without necessarily having to adhere to Hollywood's commercial diktats. In this context, McKellen has often accepted roles in films directed by emerging or little-known directors, offering not only his stage presence, but also his creative vision and professional support. On many occasions, he gave up high cachet to be part of projects that he felt were sincere and meaningful, demonstrating a rare dedication to the art of filmmaking as such, rather than to commercial success.

One of the most admirable aspects of McKellen's career in independent cinema is his commitment to supporting young talent. As one of the most respected actors in the world, McKellen has often used his fame to give visibility to up-and-coming filmmakers or projects that might otherwise have gone unnoticed. He is known to have worked with numerous young filmmakers, providing not only his talent, but also his moral and professional support, helping them find financing or promote their films at festivals. For McKellen, independent cinema is not only an opportunity to express himself as an actor, but also a way to contribute to the growth of the film industry as a whole by fostering innovation and supporting new artistic voices. This kind of generosity is uncommon in the film industry, where personal success is often put before the artistic community, but McKellen has always shown himself to be an actor who sees his career as part of a bigger picture, where collaboration and mutual support are essential.

Independent cinema has also offered McKellen the chance to explore more complex and layered characters than the roles he was often offered in big films. In projects such as 'Gods and Monsters' or 'The Dresser', McKellen was able to immerse himself in narratives that dealt with themes of identity, vulnerability, memory and loss, approaching these stories with a sensitivity that showcased his interpretative mastery. Independent cinema has allowed him to work on flawed and human characters, far from the epic heroism of Gandalf or the magnetic intensity of Magneto, but just as powerful in their telling of the frailties and weaknesses of the human soul.

Despite his notoriety, McKellen has always maintained a humble approach to his work in independent cinema, seeing each new project as an opportunity to learn and grow. His ability to move nimbly between big blockbusters and small independent films is a testament to his versatility as an actor and his constant search for new artistic challenges. McKellen has never stopped looking for stories that inspire him, proving that no matter the size of the project, what really matters is the integrity and authenticity of the narrative.

Ian McKellen has made a significant contribution to independent cinema, not only through his performances, but also through his commitment to supporting young talent and his passion for low-budget projects. His love for research cinema has led him to choose roles that often challenge convention and reflect his desire to explore authentic and profound stories. Through his work in independent cinema, McKellen has shown that the art of filmmaking can thrive away from big Hollywood budgets, and that often the most meaningful and touching stories are born in this context.

Chapter 20. Iconic and unforgettable roles

In Ian McKellen's career, there are certain roles that stand out for their importance and for the impact they have had on the collective imagination. Among them, two in particular have deeply marked modern popular culture: Gandalf in 'The Lord of the Rings' and Magneto in the 'X-Men' saga. These two characters, so different from each other, have shown McKellen's extraordinary versatility, capable of going from the wise and benevolent wizard of a fantasy world to the tormented and revolutionary mutant in a dystopian future. Thanks to these performances, McKellen not only gained international fame, but also left an indelible mark on film history, becoming synonymous with these characters for millions of fans worldwide. However, his iconic roles do not stop there. His theatrical career has been equally legendary, in particular thanks to his memorable portrayal of Richard III, a character that marked a turning point in his career, proving that McKellen was capable of tackling the classics with a freshness and power that made him one of the most respected Shakespearean actors.

The character of Gandalf, perhaps the most famous played by McKellen, has become a symbol of wisdom, courage and endurance. In the films based on J.R.R. Tolkien's novels, McKellen has been able to bring an authentic Gandalf to the screen, a figure who, while immersed in a magical world, embodies universal values that transcend the fantasy genre. McKellen made Gandalf a character who inspires trust and respect, endowed with a deep sense of justice and humanity. His performance created a complex, multi-layered figure: a wise counsellor for the hobbits, a relentless commander in battles against the forces of evil, but also an affectionate friend and travelling companion. McKellen managed to balance the epic grandeur of the character with a humanity that made him accessible and loved by viewers of all ages. The line 'Thou canst not pass!' uttered by Gandalf in the dramatic battle scene against the Balrog has become part of popular culture, becoming one of the trilogy's most iconic moments and a symbol of the fight against evil. The role of Gandalf catapulted McKellen into a new dimension of stardom, but beyond commercial success, it allowed him to demonstrate how even in a purely entertainment context, an actor can bring an emotional depth that elevates the character beyond mere narrative function.

On the other hand, the role of Magneto in the 'X-Men' saga showed a completely different face of McKellen's talent. Magneto, one of the most powerful and complex mutants in the Marvel Universe, is a character haunted by his personal history and political beliefs. A Holocaust survivor, Magneto carries the weight of the persecution he suffered and develops a radical worldview, convinced that violence is the only way to protect his species, the mutants, from discrimination and annihilation. In this sense, Magneto is a tragic character whose thirst for justice leads him to become an antagonist, but with such strong and understandable motivations that the audience cannot help but empathise with him. McKellen gave Magneto a charismatic and commanding presence, combining the character's anger and pain with a vulnerability that emerges in his relationships with old friends like Professor Xavier, played by Patrick Stewart. The chemistry between McKellen and Stewart made the rivalry between Magneto and Xavier one of the most fascinating in superhero cinema, lending an emotional intensity that elevated the 'X-Men' saga beyond the usual dynamics of the genre. McKellen's ability to make Magneto as fascinating as he is dangerous has turned the character into an icon, proving that 'villains' in superhero films can be just as deep and complex as heroes.

But if Gandalf and Magneto are the roles that consecrated McKellen to the general public, his work on 'Richard III' remains a landmark in his theatre and film career. In 1995, McKellen adapted the famous Shakespearean tragedy into a film set in an alternative fascist era, offering a new interpretation of the cruel and ambitious English king. His performance in 'Richard III' was praised for its intensity and modernity, transforming a theatre classic into a vibrant and politically charged film. McKellen's Richard is manipulative, cruel, but also incredibly charming, drawing the viewer into his world of intrigue and betrayal. The choice to set the story in a 20th century totalitarian context made the play more accessible and relevant, and McKellen once again demonstrated his ability to make classic characters contemporary and universal. Richard III is a character that requires an extraordinary emotional range, moving from betrayed brotherly love to obsession with power, and McKellen masterfully captured every nuance.

McKellen's impact in the collective imagination goes beyond individual roles. His career has been marked by a constant search for new ways to express the human condition through the characters he plays, and his dedication to the art of acting has inspired generations of actors and spectators. Besides his extraordinary versatility, what makes McKellen unique is his ability to find humanity in even the most fantastic or evil roles, making each character believable and complex. His Gandalf and Magneto are not simply heroes or antagonists, but figures that reflect deep moral and personal conflicts, and resonate with the audience on an emotional level. This ability to transcend genre and bring a deep authenticity to each role has made McKellen a central figure not only in the world of film and theatre, but also in global popular culture.

Ian McKellen has built an extraordinary career through a series of iconic and unforgettable roles, proving that a great actor can make his mark in blockbusters as well as theatrical classics. His ability to blend power and sensitivity, to play epic and tragic characters with equal intensity, has ensured that his work remains etched in the collective memory. From the battlefields of Middle-earth to the intricate political plots of the English kingdom, McKellen has turned each role into an opportunity to explore the human condition, leaving a legacy that will continue to influence the imagination of generations to come.

Chapter 21. The contribution to modern theatre

Ian McKellen has made a fundamental contribution to modern theatre, proving that an actor's greatness is not only measured by his presence on the big screen, but above all by his ability to influence and transform theatre, both in terms of performance and cultural engagement. His career, which has spanned decades of theatrical evolution, has seen McKellen become not only one of the greatest interpreters of Shakespeare's classics, but also a reference point for the new generation of actors, a figure capable of bringing classical theatre into the contemporary era without ever losing sight of the importance of the text and authenticity in acting. His love for the theatre has been evident since his early days, and even today, after a career full of film successes, McKellen continues to return to the stage, testifying to an unwavering dedication and passion that knows no bounds.

One of the most influential aspects of McKellen's contribution to contemporary theatre has been his constant return to the classics, particularly Shakespeare, whose work has been a constant throughout his career. At a time when theatre often tends to seek out new forms of experimentation or re-present the classics in an overly detached manner, McKellen has shown how the works of Shakespeare and other great playwrights can still speak to contemporary audiences when interpreted with honesty and depth. Through his portrayal of iconic roles such as Hamlet, Macbeth, Richard III and King Lear, McKellen has shown how these characters can still explore the universal dilemmas of the human soul: power, madness, love, revenge and mortality. Each of his interpretations was a journey into the psychology of the characters, bringing to the stage multifaceted versions in which the emotional complexity of the texts translated into vibrant and powerful acting that left no room for superficiality. His work has influenced the way in which many modern directors and actors have approached the classics, pushing them to seek authenticity and depth, rather than focusing only on stage effect.

McKellen has always believed that theatre should be accessible to all, and not an art reserved for a cultural elite. This is reflected in his choice to perform in productions that reach a wide audience, participating in international and national tours with theatre companies such as the Royal Shakespeare Company and the National Theatre, but also in smaller, more intimate projects in which he has performed in more modest spaces. For McKellen, theatre is an art form that can profoundly influence society, and this has been seen in his efforts to bring Shakespeare to schools, local theatres and even outdoors, with the aim of bringing new generations closer to texts that might otherwise seem distant and incomprehensible. He has often argued that theatre should not just be a performance, but a means to better understand ourselves and the world around us, an opportunity to reflect on universal issues that cut across the ages.

McKellen's relationship with the new generation of actors is another crucial aspect of his contribution to modern theatre. As a leading figure in the acting world, McKellen has often taken on the role of mentor for young actors, offering advice, support and inspiration. His generosity in sharing his knowledge is well known in theatre circles, and many emerging actors have benefited from his guidance, learning not only the art of acting, but also respect for the text and the audience. McKellen has always emphasised the importance of discipline and commitment in acting, remembering that the actor is first and foremost a servant of the text and that theatre requires total dedication, a dedication that does not end with celebrity or personal success. Thanks to this vision, many young actors who have had the opportunity to work with McKellen consider him to be a true master, someone who was able to convey not only a love of theatre, but also a work ethic that is rare today in an industry often dominated by image and the market.

McKellen's influence on modern theatre goes beyond his personal performance. His career has helped redefine the role of the Shakespearean actor in contemporary times, proving that classical theatre can also be relevant and fascinating to modern audiences. He has shown how Shakespeare does not have to be revered as a relic of the past, but can be reinterpreted and experienced in a new and dynamic way, without betraying the essence of the text. This approach has influenced directors, actors and theatre companies around the world, who have looked to McKellen as an example of how an actor can bring innovation and freshness to even the most traditional plays.

In addition to his impact on classic productions, McKellen has played a key role in promoting theatre as a space for inclusivity and diversity. His public commitment to LGBTQ+ rights and equality has also been reflected in his theatre work, both in the choice of projects in which he has participated and in the way he has used theatre as a platform to promote social change. McKellen has often emphasised the importance of theatre as a place for discussion and representation of diverse human identities, and has worked to advance this vision, both through his direct involvement in productions and through his support of other theatre initiatives that aim to promote diversity. This commitment has had a significant impact not only on the theatre world, but also on society at large, showing how art can be a tool for change and social reflection.

Ian McKellen's theatrical legacy will endure. Thanks to his work, many actors today feel inspired to seek the truth in the characters they play, to explore the text with honesty and to always put the audience at the centre of their performance. McKellen has shown that theatre is a living, evolving art that can speak to every generation if approached with passion and respect. His influence extends far beyond the stage, helping to shape a new generation of artists who see theatre not just as a means of entertainment, but as a vehicle for change and exploration of the human soul. Ian McKellen has left an indelible mark on modern theatre, and his ongoing commitment to this art form is a beacon for anyone wishing to understand the transformative power of theatre.

Chapter 22. The artistic legacy of Ian McKellen

Ian McKellen's artistic legacy is destined to leave a deep and lasting mark on both the film and theatre worlds. Throughout his long career, McKellen has demonstrated extraordinary versatility and talent, embodying iconic roles that have spanned generations, genres and formats, from Shakespearean acting on stage to blockbuster films. His impact on the acting world goes beyond technical prowess or interpretative skill: McKellen has set new standards of excellence, not only for his ability to bring complex and layered characters to life, but also for his passion and dedication to the art of acting. His influence extends far beyond his individual performances, inspiring thousands of actors, directors and emerging artists to follow his example of commitment, authenticity and creative curiosity.

One of the most significant aspects of McKellen's legacy is the way he has embodied classical theatre, particularly Shakespeare, and brought it into the 21st century. His interpretations of characters such as Macbeth, Richard III, King Lear and Hamlet have redefined the way these roles are perceived by modern audiences. His ability to breathe new life into ancient texts, to make them current and relevant without distorting their depth, has shown that classical theatre can still speak to contemporary generations. McKellen has been able to embody the universal power of Shakespeare's texts, showing that the themes addressed by the Bard - such as the thirst for power, madness, love, revenge - are eternally valid and echo in today's society. This approach has had a profound impact on directors and actors, who look to him as a master capable of fusing tradition and modernity in one extraordinary performance. Many emerging artists, inspired by his work, have approached the classics with renewed energy and respect, recognising that there is always something new to discover in ancient works when they are treated with passion and authenticity.

McKellen has not only elevated classical theatre, he has also been able to move with extreme agility between the stage and the silver screen, creating a bridge between two worlds often perceived as separate. His ability to move from theatre to film without losing the depth of his acting has inspired an entire generation of actors to consider their artistic career as a journey in which there are no barriers between the various means of expression. His film roles, from Gandalf in 'Lord of the Rings' to Magneto in 'X-Men', have become part of the global collective imagination, leading McKellen to be recognised not only as a great Shakespearean actor, but also as a true icon of popular culture. In these roles, he has shown that even in genres such as fantasy or superhero movies, often seen as lighter than drama, one can bring an emotional intensity and psychological depth that transform characters into memorable and universal figures. Gandalf, with his wisdom and courage, and Magneto, with his tragic charisma and struggle for survival, are not just heroes or antagonists: thanks to McKellen's mastery, they have become complex and layered symbols, capable of speaking to audiences of all ages and cultures.

McKellen's ability to cross genres and mediums has helped redefine the concept of the contemporary actor. He has never accepted being labelled or limited to a particular type of role, but has constantly challenged himself, exploring new territories and experimenting with the most diverse characters. His approach has paved the way for a new generation of actors who see acting as a fluid and ever-evolving art, in which it is possible to range across genres, formats and styles without ever losing one's artistic identity. McKellen demonstrated that the art of acting is first and foremost a matter of authenticity and emotional depth, regardless of the context. This message has had a strong impact on actors around the world, who see him as a role model not only for his skill, but also for his work ethic and his willingness to continue to learn and grow.

In addition to his direct influence on acting, McKellen's legacy is also reflected in his contribution to popular culture. His characters have entered the pantheon of iconic figures in film and television, becoming reference points for generations of viewers. His work has shown that highly entertaining films can have a high artistic quality and that even seemingly 'genre' characters can carry an emotional and intellectual depth. Gandalf and Magneto, for instance, are not mere fictional figures: they are symbols of inner and social struggles, embodiments of universal values that resonate deeply with audiences. McKellen has interpreted these characters with such intensity and humanity that they have become an integral part of popular culture, influencing the way people perceive good, evil, wisdom and rebellion.

Another key aspect of McKellen's legacy is his commitment to diversity and inclusiveness in the world of entertainment. His activism for LGBTQ+ rights and his fight against all forms of discrimination have helped to create a more open and welcoming environment for artists of all identities. McKellen has always used his fame and visibility to advance social justice battles, proving that an actor is not only a performer, but also a citizen of the world with a responsibility to promote change. His courage in speaking openly about his sexuality, at a time when doing so entailed personal and professional risks, has inspired countless artists to be themselves and fight for their rights. His commitment has had a profound impact not only in the entertainment world, but also in society at large, helping to change the way issues of identity and equality are perceived.

Ian McKellen's artistic legacy goes far beyond his performances on stage or screen. His impact is reflected in the way he has transformed theatre and film, inspiring a new generation of artists to explore their own authenticity and to always seek truth in the characters they play. He has shown that success does not have to limit artistic ambition, and that fame can be used to do good, to give a voice to those who do not have one, and to promote a fairer, more inclusive world. McKellen has left an indelible mark on contemporary culture, and his influence will continue to be felt for many years to come, both through his iconic roles and his personal commitment to a fairer and more accessible art for all.

---Conclusion---

Throughout his career, Ian McKellen has built a legacy that transcends show business, becoming a symbolic and charismatic figure in both theatre and film. His roles, from intricate Shakespearean tragic figures to iconic pop culture characters such as Gandalf and Magneto, have redefined the concept of acting versatility. But what makes him truly unique is not just his ability to play such diverse characters, but the depth with which he tackles each role. Each of his performances is a total immersion in the character, a relentless search for the emotional and psychological truth that makes each figure he plays believable and human, leading the audience to reflect, be moved and explore new horizons.

McKellen's contribution is not limited to his prowess on stage or in front of the camera. As an activist for LGBTQ+ rights, he has played a key role in the fight for equality and social justice. His courage in coming out openly gay at a time when many feared the repercussions of such a gesture inspired millions, proving that authenticity is a powerful force not only on stage, but also in real life. Thanks to his commanding voice, McKellen has become a reference point for those fighting against discrimination, using his celebrity to give visibility to important causes and to promote social change that has had a global impact.

In addition to activism, his unwavering commitment to making theatre and film accessible to a wider audience has profoundly influenced the entertainment industry. McKellen has always believed that art should be experienced by all, regardless of social, economic or cultural barriers. His ability to bring Shakespeare to schools, local theatres and even cinemas around the world has brought millions of people closer to the great theatre tradition, proving that classical theatre is not just for a small elite, but can speak to every generation. This inclusive vision of the art has opened new doors for many young actors and directors who now follow his example, striving to create theatre and cinema that is truly for everyone. Ian McKellen's legacy is that of a man who was able to use his talent, his voice and his celebrity to make the world a better place, both through art and through his civic engagement. His impact on the world of acting, his influence on future generations and his contribution to popular culture will forever be etched in history. But perhaps his greatest legacy is the example of a man who, despite his success and fame, never stopped seeking truth, integrity and justice, both on stage and in his everyday life. Ian McKellen taught the world that being a great actor also means being a great person, capable of leaving a mark not only through the characters he plays, but also through the actions he performs and the values he defends.

Ian McKellen: Extraordinary Life and Career

The official tribute to the world's theatre and film icon

Henry Lyle Donovan

Made in the USA
Columbia, SC
04 February 2025